# Contents

# Foreword

When the *Community Care Handbook* was first written, the community care reforms were about to be implemented. There was widespread anxiety and uncertainty about how people receiving community care would be affected by the proposed changes. The book therefore aimed to explain the new system, as set out in the White Paper *Caring for People* and enacted in the NHS and Community Care Act 1990. It was felt that the transition was likely to be smoother if the people who provided community care understood the nature and purpose of the new arrangements.

Nearly two years on the need for an explanation of the community care reforms remains. People become involved with community care from a wide range of backgrounds: many new staff of all types may have no prior experience in health or social care. In addition, many who are already involved in providing community care, for example a care home manager or someone working in a local authority housing department, may be familiar with only a few aspects of the reforms: they may benefit greatly from an understanding of the broad framework. Even those who are familiar with the broad framework of the reforms may need from time to time to 'go back to basics'. Focusing just on assessments or funding – as many people have in recent months – may divert attention from other aspects of the reforms, such as new inspection systems, which should contribute to improved quality of care for older people. This underlying aim of the reforms means that it is entirely appropriate that the second edition of the *Community Care Handbook* be published by Age Concern England.

For all such people the new edition of the *Community Care Handbook* looks at the background to the community care legislation and explains the reforms themselves in detail. In doing so it makes extensive reference to guidance issued by the Government to local and health authorities on implementation of the reforms.

In many ways a complicated subject has become even more so as local and health authorities all over the country have pursued very different ways of implementing the reforms. This second edition of the *Community Care Handbook* aims to make clearer what is happening in different parts of the country.

However, the book is more than just an explanation of the new system and its origins. Throughout its pages it aims to remind the reader of the importance of focusing on the person – on the individual older people whose experience of community care will be determined not only by the rules and regulations but also by the attitudes of all those who work for and with older people, and who plan and purchase services on their behalf. Those who work within the system need to understand how it should work, but they also need to remind themselves continually of the importance of 'remembering the person' – the theme of the book's final chapter.

**Sally Greengross**
*Director General, Age Concern England*

# About the author

Barbara Meredith is a Senior Policy and Development Officer at the National Consumer Council. From 1987 to 1994 she was an Information and Policy Officer at Age Concern England, where her work centred on the community care reforms and on issues related to the funding and provision of long-term care for older people.

Educated in her native USA, Barbara Meredith studied Government at Cornell University before coming to live in England. She has an MSc (Econ) in Social Administration from the London School of Economics.

As an adult education teacher, Barbara Meredith worked with adults returning to study, as well as teaching examination courses in welfare rights and social administration. Her interest in services for and policies about older people has been sustained through welfare rights work, and through involvement in research projects at the London School of Economics and at the Policy Studies Institute. She is the author of *A Selected Bibliography of Social Planning for the Elderly*, published by the Centre for Policy on Ageing; and co-author with Susan Tester of *Ill-informed? A study of information and support for elderly people in the inner city* (Policy Studies Institute), and with Jane Lewis of *Daughters Who Care* (Routledge).

Barbara Meredith was a member of the Wagner Development Group, which took forward the recommendations of the Wagner Report on residential care.

# Acknowledgements

The preparation of this book has involved many colleagues and former colleagues from Age Concern England and the wider Age Concern movement. These include David Bookbinder, Michael Boyd, Jane Jones, David Moncrieff, Mary Rutherford, Robin Versteeg, Sally West, Jane Whelan, Lorna Easterbrook and Richard Wood. Vinnette Marshall has had the complex task of word processing successive versions of the text. Evelyn McEwen, Bob Anderson and Shelagh Doonan have provided detailed and helpful comments on the first draft of the second edition; Caroline Hartnell has exercised tremendous skill in editing, always with sympathetic and tactful support.

The responsibility for factual accuracy and for opinions expressed in the book rests with me. All names used in examples are fictitious.

I have received invaluable insights about how the community care reforms are developing from social services and Age Concern personnel in several counties and metropolitan boroughs. I am grateful for the time which they shared with me.

Personal experience also enriches my view of community care. Community care is part of all our lives. It would be impossible to write about it without being influenced by the experiences of relatives, friends and neighbours, and the older people and their support organisations with whom I work. Their experiences are the litmus test of the quality of community care.

**Barbara Meredith**
*January 1995*

# Preface to the first edition

Since joining Age Concern in 1987, I have been working on aspects of the community care reforms. I therefore welcomed the opportunity to write a book explaining the reforms to people who have not been privileged over the years to follow them in minute detail.

The reforms are complex and far-reaching. Not everyone agrees with every part of them, but they are here to stay. It is important that everyone involved with community care understands how they work, and what some of their effects might be. The aim of this book is to make the changes more understandable. Chapters 1–8 describe the history of community care and explain the current changes. Chapter 9 reflects on aspects of the changes and the 'ideals' of community care.

The examples in the book are about older people, but much of the text will relate to most adults who need care.

This book describes the provisions of the White Paper, *Caring for People*, and Part III of the NHS and Community Care Act 1990 in England. In Wales, the provisions of Part III of the Act apply, but there are differences from England in how the reforms are carried out. Separate sections of the White Paper and the Act apply to Scotland and are not dealt with in this book, nor is the situation in Northern Ireland, which was covered by neither the Act nor the White Paper. The changes mainly involve local authority social services departments. (In Scotland, services are organised slightly differently. Social services are provided by social work departments, and some arrangements are different from those in England and Wales.)

# Preface to the second edition

When the first edition of this book was written, the community care changes had only partially begun. Since the full implementation of the reforms in April 1993, there have been changes in procedures and practice which are noted in this second edition.

All aspects of the reforms have been monitored by the Department of Health (through the Social Services Inspectorate and Regional Health Authorities) and by other organisations, including university research departments, independent consultants, the Audit Commission and voluntary organisations such as Age Concern and the Carers National Association. This book does not include all the detail of such studies, but aims to indicate the broad themes of their findings.

Writing about the reforms was considerably easier before they got fully under way than nearly two years down the road. The lack of central standards, the incredible variation among local and health authorities, the continued reform of the National Health Service, future reform of some local authorities, and concerns about funding, all add to the complexity of any analysis of the effect of the reforms.

In general there is no conclusive picture of the success to date of the reforms as a whole, nor of that of their component parts, as described in Chapters 3–7 of this book. Monitoring reports have shown that implementation has been very varied in different parts of the country. In some places, considerable successes can be identified with some parts of the reforms, while other areas face problems. There are several reasons for this, which include:

- No national standards for implementation were set by the Government. Local authorities have therefore used many different ways to bring about the reforms. It is difficult to compare and contrast very different systems.

- There was little 'baseline' information about provision of services before the reforms. It is therefore difficult to say whether some service improvements are a direct result of the reforms or would have happened anyway.

- Other changes have taken place which may affect the success of the reforms themselves, such as the continuing reform and reorganisation of the NHS, and changes in the provision of NHS long-term nursing care.

Although the community care reforms have happened alongside major changes in the health service, the two systems remain separate in almost every way. As explained in Chapter 1, they are governed by different laws, have different structures and funding systems, and have both undergone major reform. Yet the success of the community care reforms depends to a great extent on successful links between social services and health care. As far as possible, these links are mentioned when the reforms themselves are looked at, but the book focuses mainly on the social services aspects of the reforms.

This book is not intended as a policy discussion of the reforms. It aims – as did the first edition – to help the reader to understand the reforms, their place in the overall context of community care, and some of the issues surrounding the provision of health, social and other care services for older people.

Finally, the reader is reminded that the system as set out in *Caring for People* covers mainly those aspects of 'community care' which are controlled by social services and, to a lesser extent, health and housing. The Griffiths Report, and more recently the House of Commons Health Select Committee and the Association of Directors of Social Services,[1] recommended that there should be a formal means for central government to monitor how its different policies *together* affect community care. These would include policies for pensions, disability, benefits, fuel costs and other subjects. To date the Government has not taken formal action in this respect.

# Introduction

## ANNIE – A CASE STUDY IN COMMUNITY CARE

When Annie broke her hip, her carefully balanced world seemed to fall apart. She had managed the problems of Parkinson's disease with help from her family and neighbours, and she could still tend the garden if she moved slowly. Grandchildren came to stay, and her son and daughter visited regularly. She baked for her neighbour, in exchange for help in the garden and with heavy chores.

All that changed one summer afternoon when she tripped over the garden hose. Three months later, she was home from hospital with a new hip, and a new routine. The home help came several times a week at first, then less. Meals on wheels was started, but the food was unappetising, and the person who delivered the meals simply dashed in and out – not even time to say hello. This made Annie feel uncomfortable, and she decided not to continue with the meals.

The physiotherapist helped her learn to walk again, and she gradually gained strength. She worked hard to regain confidence, but her family were worried about how she would continue to cope with the stairs and a house which was really too large.

Sheltered flats were being built nearby. Her family urged Annie to move there, so that she could be on one floor, with help if she needed it. But Annie didn't feel able to face the upheaval. She had good neighbours, and she didn't want to give up the garden, or the space in case the grandchildren came to stay.

The boy next door took her shopping every week – until he went away to college. His mother had gone to work full time, so she wasn't around so much either. In the second year after her fall, Annie stayed in all winter, not even sitting in the garden when the warmer weather came. She fell frequently, but the alarm promised by the Council had never been put in, and she worried about how she would get help if she needed it. Her son and daughter both had families and full-time jobs.

Two years after her fall, Annie fell and lay for several hours unable to move. She said she couldn't go on with the fear of falling, and she quickly made arrangements to go into a nearby residential home. She didn't really need 'care' – so much as support. She was quite capable of cooking her own meals and doing most things for herself, but once she was in the home, she didn't really need to any more. She was lovingly cared for, but had little opportunity to do much for herself. Her spirits and her abilities gradually declined.

As her illness progressed, Annie grew increasingly afraid about what might happen to her. She began to fall more frequently, and the home's owners warned her that she might not be able to stay if she became too dependent. Two years after entering the home, Annie relapsed, becoming bedridden and confused. In her lucid moments, she told her daughter that she wished she didn't have to carry on. The last few weeks of her life were spent peacefully and securely in a geriatric hospital.

Annie was a user of 'community care'. Her story happened before the community care reforms. Before and after her fall she was supported in many ways by her family and neighbours. After she had her new hip, she was helped by nurses, the home help, the physiotherapist, and by meals on wheels, although the hoped-for alarm never materialised.

It wasn't as if she needed all that much care; but it didn't seem to be put together so that she felt confident staying at home. Her family found it hard to persuade her to consider living in a more suitable home, and there wasn't anyone else who had the time to help her to make that decision. Once Annie was in the care home, it was as if the 'community' was far away, even though she was only half a mile from her former home.

This book is about community care. It is written for the many people who may be involved in helping to provide community care for people like Annie. It will describe:

- what community care is, and why it is so important;
- the kinds of people who may need community care;
- the people and the organisations which may be involved in providing community care;
- the changes which took place from 1991 to 1993 in the provision and funding of some community care services and how these have worked;
- developments following the implementation of the reforms in April 1993.

According to the Government the aim of community care is to help people with care needs to live as independent a life as possible in their own homes for as long as this is reasonable and practical. Yet this is not an easy task. The story of Annie illustrates good and bad aspects of the way community care can work in practice: how easy it is to be in too much of a hurry to stop and talk; how much neighbours and friends can help, yet how difficult it is to depend on them given that their circumstances may change and they may not be able to help any more; how hard it sometimes seems to organise little things which might make a big difference – like an alarm; and how difficult it is for people to plan how they will deal with their own frailty.

The community care reforms aim to help people find appropriate care through careful assessment and clear statements about what support is available in each area of the country. They are meant to create a system which protects the interests of users of services and raises the quality of services. Whether these changes succeed depends partly on the amount of money available to carry them out, and on the availability of appropriate health care, housing and other factors. However, success also depends on the attitudes of all the people involved. The changes are complex and not always easy to understand. Many people have only the vaguest idea of what is happening. Yet everyone who is working 'in the community' needs to have some understanding of how the reformed system works.

Readers should be warned that this book describes a constantly changing scene. It aims to provide the essential background information which people need if they are to begin to understand the principles of the reformed system, but its subject matter is not set in stone. If the book improves understanding, and stimulates further thought and reflection, it will have succeeded in its objectives.

# 1 What is Community Care?

'Community care' has no single meaning. Broadly it means helping people who need care and support to live with dignity and as much independence as possible 'in the community'. The 'community' is hard to define. It most often means ordinary homes – but for some people it includes special forms of housing, or residential or nursing homes.

New arrangements have been introduced for publicly provided social services. These are often referred to as the 'community care reforms'. They were first described in a 1989 Government document called *Caring for People*. The NHS and Community Care Act 1990 made the necessary legal changes, which were fully implemented in April 1993.

It is important not to equate these 'community care reforms' with 'community care'. This tends to happen partly because people have taken to referring to the reforms as 'implementing community care', even talking about April 1993 as 'when community care came in'. As we show in Chapter 2, community care has been around for many years.

## WHAT ARE THE COMMUNITY CARE REFORMS?

The reforms introduced new procedures for arranging and paying for state-funded social care. They are described in Chapters 3–8. Broadly, the Government has stated that they aim to:

- make the best use of public money – to make sure that the services which are provided by local and health authorities are provided for those who need them most, and actually meet their needs;

- encourage authorities to set priorities – to decide how they will spend money if there is not enough to provide for everyone's needs;

- ensure that local authorities check on the quality of care which is being provided – through inspection units, complaints procedures, care management, setting service specifications and monitoring contracts for care;

- encourage local authorities to use other organisations to provide services – not just to provide them themselves.

Before looking at the background to the changes, this chapter looks at the varied nature of community care – at who may use it, and at the different service providers.

# WHAT IS COMMUNITY CARE?

Community care is like a jigsaw puzzle. It is the combination of support and services for a person with care needs. These include provision which is largely outside the scope of this book, such as pensions, benefits and income; transport; housing; the opportunity to work; policies for essential services, such as fuel and telephones; recreation, education and leisure.

The meaning of community care will depend on each person's needs:

**Fred Upton** is 69. He has lived for 48 years in a large mental handicap hospital which is being closed. As part of the closure programme, Mr Upton has been taking part in training to help him learn to manage outside the hospital. He is going to live in a small group home with some of his friends from hospital. They are going to live 'in the community'.

**Mrs Prashar** is 72. She has no children, and no relatives nearby. She has had a stroke and walks with a frame. After a period of rehabilitation in hospital, she has returned to her own home. She has a battery-operated wheelchair in which she goes to the local shops. A nurse comes in the morning to help her get dressed, a home help sees to the cleaning, and her neighbour calls in several times a day and last thing at night. Mrs Prashar is living 'in the community'. She is a user of 'community care'.

**John and Iris O'Donnell** live in a block of flats in the inner city. Mrs O'Donnell has never gone out very much, and has few friends. She is becoming increasingly confused. She forgets to wash herself, and can't cook any more. Mr O'Donnell is upset about this, but doesn't know what to do. He does the shopping and the cooking, but finds the personal care for his wife increasingly difficult and embarrassing. Mr and Mrs O'Donnell live 'in the community', but they do not appear to be benefiting from 'community care'.

Community care is part of our lives. It is the web of care and support provided for frail, sick or dependent people both by their families or other members of the community and by public or other services.

This means helping some people remain in their homes, or creating homelike places with appropriate support. In general, community care means a preference for home life over 'institutional care'. It means helping people to be 'integrated' with their local community rather than being separate from it, perhaps in a large long-stay hospital. Where people do live with others – in what are called 'communal' settings or 'group homes' – there is a general preference for smaller homes, close to where people have always lived.

# Where is 'home'?

While it is generally agreed that community care means helping people to live the life of their choice, given their particular illness or disabilities, and preferably in their own homes, defining 'home' is not a simple matter. People with different needs may find appropriate care in different places. Each of these is 'home' to the person who lives there. Examples of these include:

- a hostel or group home, for people who have been discharged from a long-stay hospital – perhaps with a support worker living in, or calling in regularly;
- the family home for a child with learning disabilities, later followed by a move to independent living, or to a small group home;
- a specially adapted house or flat for someone with physical disabilities;
- a residential or nursing home;
- a hospital, if that is where the person lives and the care there is appropriate to that person's needs (it is fair to say that most definitions of 'the community' do not include hospitals, but there is no reason why

someone who lives in a long-stay hospital should be excluded from 'the community');

■ a 'sheltered' or 'retirement' home, with support from a warden and perhaps some extra care services available;

■ a family home, which provides 'foster' or 'family-based' care for one or more people.

Physically living in one's own home does not necessarily mean a good quality of life. For some people, living on their own may mean that they have less care and fewer friends than they might have in a communal home.

One dilemma of community care is how to get the balance right between helping people remain in their homes and not forcing them to do so when it is not their wish, or it is no longer possible for them to have a good quality of life at home.

## What does community care involve?

Most community care is provided by family, neighbours and friends, although many people do not have such support. The ideal is that this care should be backed up where necessary by services which are appropriate for the needs of the people being cared for and their carers.

Although such services are organised differently in each area, users of services have some universal needs, including:

**Information**
To enable them to find out what is available, and from whom.

**Practical support**
Equipment, or adaptations to their homes, to help cope with particular disabilities.

**Domestic assistance**
To help with the tasks of everyday life.

**Emotional support**
To help them come to terms with their particular problem.

**Physical and/or nursing care**
To help with their illness or disability.

**Financial support**
To maintain a reasonable quality of life, and help to compensate for the costs of disability and, for many people, the loss of or reduction in earnings.

**Appropriate housing**
A warm and affordable place to live.

**Access to transport**
The ability to take part in community life.

**Access to recreation and leisure and work.**
Appropriate provision in all these respects should contribute to a better *quality of life* for the person with community care needs. What is appropriate will depend not only on the person's needs, but also on his or her expectations and personal preferences.

# WHO USES COMMUNITY CARE?

Ordinary people use community care. They are people who happen to have special needs which mean that they cannot cope in one way or another with their own care. They may be ill, have a physical or mental disability, be unable to perform some everyday tasks – like bathing or cleaning – or have lived for too many years in the limited environment of an institution.

Such people are often referred to in terms of 'client groups'. This is a kind of shorthand which focuses on the particular characteristics of groups of people. There is, however, a danger in thinking about people as belonging to client groups: in general, people do not think of themselves as carrying such a label.

**A 78-year-old woman in hospital**, after a hip replacement: 'The doctor came round yesterday with a group of students. He stood at the door and said, "These are my geriatrics." But *I'm* not geriatric.'

For planners and providers of services, it can be easy to forget that service users are unique individuals, each with their own needs and their own hopes. This applies to 'residents' of care homes, 'clients' of home care services, or 'the blind', 'the deaf' or 'the homeless' – all different people who happen to share similar circumstances or places of care. This definitely does not make them all the same. In thinking about the community care reforms we must constantly remind ourselves not to become so bogged down in *process* that we forget the people for whom the care is intended. Each part of the process should be based firmly on what users of different services want for themselves.

Yet in order to plan for services it is convenient, perhaps necessary, to think of service users in terms of client groups. Keeping the balance between planning for groups of people and helping individuals with particular and unique needs is a great challenge.

Another way of reminding ourselves that we are talking about *people* is to remember to use that word when we talk about the client groups. Thus it is important to talk about 'elderly – or older – people' rather than 'the elderly'; or 'people with mental health problems', rather than 'the mentally ill'. There used to be a Minister for the Disabled. This title has been changed to 'Minister for Disabled People'. This may seem rather trivial, but it is a recognition that groups with special needs are made up of individual people.

# Adult client groups

There are a number of adult 'client groups'. (This book does not cover children, whose needs include education as well as other aspects of community care. The Children Act 1989 has introduced many changes relevant to provision for children and their protection.) Adult client groups include:

## Elderly people

This term generally refers to people aged 65 or over – or to people over pension age, which is currently 60 for women and 65 for men. The 'elderly client group' covers an age span of 40 or more years. In 1992 there were 9,138,000 people aged 65 or over in the UK and 10.6 million over pension age.

Ageing is not a disease, and it does not automatically produce ill health. However, as we age we are more likely to experience chronic illnesses or conditions which can lead to a need for care. A survey of disability in Great Britain[2] found that almost 70 per cent of disabled adults were aged

60 or over, and nearly half were aged 70 or over. Forty per cent of the most severely disabled adults were aged 80 or over, and it is estimated that there will be nearly 1.2 million people aged 85 or over by the year 2001. It is these people who are most likely to need community care – although such generalisations mask the fact that many younger elderly people need care, while many very elderly people need no care at all.

Some care for elderly people is called 'geriatric' care. This word is most often used in the health services to refer to people over a certain age – perhaps 75 or 80. Geriatrics is a medical specialty which focuses on improving the situation of elderly people with illnesses or disabilities, taking into account all the medical and social factors needed for their care. Elderly people themselves do not always like to be referred to as 'geriatrics', as we have seen.

## People with physical disabilities

People with physical disabilities can be of any age, but older age groups include larger proportions of people with physical disabilities than younger age groups. Physical disabilities may develop gradually, as with arthritis or degenerative changes to the spine, or suddenly, as with a stroke. Some mental illnesses or handicaps also cause physical problems; people with advanced Alzheimer's disease may, for instance, have problems walking.

## People with mental health problems

There is a wide range of mental illnesses, which affect people of all ages. Some are readily treated with medication; others respond to counselling and various types of therapy. Some, such as Alzheimer's disease, are progressive diseases as a result of which the patient's condition will gradually deteriorate. One in five people over the age of 80 is thought to be likely to develop this condition. If the actual numbers of this age group are rising, then there will be an increase in the numbers of people with Alzheimer's disease.

Surveys show that something between 11 and 14 per cent of people aged 65 or over suffer from depression, a condition which is not always properly diagnosed.

Sometimes there is special reference to a client group known as 'elderly mentally ill', or EMI. Another group is referred to as ESMI – 'elderly severely mentally ill'. 'Psychogeriatrics' refers to specialist care for elderly people with mental illness.

## People with learning disabilities

(Formerly referred to as mentally handicapped people, or people with mental handicap, and sometimes referred to as people with learning difficulties.) At one time people with learning disabilities were most often cared for in long-stay hospitals. Now, as children, they live mainly with their parents; as adults, they should be helped to live in supported settings, if they so wish.

Some people with learning disabilities still live in long-stay institutions, where they were sent many years ago. At the same time, those in the community are living much longer than they once did. As their parents grow older, they become increasingly concerned to ensure that their children are well cared for after they die or become too frail to continue caring for them.

In recent years, people with learning disabilities have been helped through advocacy schemes to have more of a say about how they would like to live (see p 86).

---

**NORMALISATION**

'Normalisation' is the word often used to describe the principles of care for people with learning disabilities or people with mental health problems. Such people 'may be viewed as objects of pity and charity; as violent and dangerous; as sick; or as subhuman "vegetables". Because of this they have become devalued in society; they are segregated from other people and denied the most basic human rights. They are treated as second-class citizens.

'Normalisation . . . suggests ways of offering services which support people in becoming valued members of society. It is not about "making people normal" – the most common misinterpretation of the principle . . .'[3]

---

## People with drug or alcohol problems

Care for these people may involve counselling, treatment programmes or specialist supported housing or homes. Treatment and support may be more directive than in other forms of community care.

## People with HIV or AIDS

Care, support and counselling are all vital to people who are HIV positive or who develop AIDS, and their carers. Such people may have some things in common with people who are terminally ill.

## People who are terminally ill

Hospice care, with its special emphasis on improving the quality of dying, is most often thought of in relation to cancer patients. However, such care can be relevant for people in the final stages of other illnesses and conditions. It can be provided in a hospice or in a person's own home. The final stages of Alzheimer's disease have been called a 'living bereavement' for relatives because of the changed character and heavy care needs of the person suffering from the disease.

## Homeless people

People with no permanent address often have difficulty finding help from care services. This could be because they are reluctant to seek help, or because they cannot find anyone willing to care for them. Many single homeless people suffer from mental illness, and the problems of older homeless people are increasingly causing concern. Homelessness is the extreme end of housing need. Housing is of great importance for all client groups.

## Discrimination in care provision

Lumping people into categories may adversely affect the kind of treatment or services they receive. A person aged 65 or over could be physically disabled and have a mental illness. If he or she is treated mainly as being 'elderly mentally ill', they may not be thought of as eligible for services which are meant mainly for people who have physical disabilities. Services for people with mental health problems may include counselling, which may not be on offer to people who are labelled as '*elderly* mentally ill'. These are forms of 'age discrimination' or 'ageism'. According to a Medical Research Council report,[4] age discrimination is increasingly evident in health care, where decisions are frequently taken on the basis of age alone, rather than the physiological state of the patient.

Other forms of discrimination have to do with a person's sex or race. It is sometimes wrongly believed that people from black and ethnic minority communities do not need services because they 'look after their own'. In most cases, it is much more likely that services are not offered in a way which is understandable to people whose first language is not English, or which are acceptable to people with different customs or religions. Community care services need to guard against such discrimination and cater for all the communities in an area. They should be developed with and by the people who need them. Services imposed on any group of people are likely to be inappropriate.

## A range of policies

To some extent, the concept of 'community care' differs according to the particular person or group of people being discussed at any moment, although the basic principles should be common across client groups. The phrase can be confusing, however, as policies for client groups may emphasise different things. Following some tragic incidents involving people with severe mental health problems, for instance, there has been considerable public and media concern about 'community care' for such people. But even here the focus is different for the relatively small number of people with severe mental health problems and the much larger group who need perhaps intermittent but long-term support to enable them to live successful lives in the community.

Rather than thinking of 'community care' as a single, all-embracing concept, it is perhaps preferable to regard it as a *range* of policies, with variable application depending on the client group or type of care being discussed.

# WHO PROVIDES COMMUNITY CARE?

## Carers

We have seen that most community care is provided by family, friends and neighbours. Such people are often referred to as 'informal carers', to distinguish them from people who work in the 'formal' sectors – public, private and voluntary services. It should be noted that many carers do not like the use of the word 'informal' to refer to the work they do.

A 1990 OPCS survey concluded that some 6.8 million people in Britain offer some form of support to people with care needs; 1.5 million carers offer more than 20 hours per week of care. Of these, 28 per cent are aged 65 or over. Many older carers are spouses, and many report that they themselves have some form of long-standing illness.[5]

### THE NEEDS OF CARERS

Carers are people of all ages who support people with an infinite variety of needs. Carers want to be listened to, and believe that their needs must be considered alongside those of the people they care for. They want to be recognised for the contribution they make to the overall pattern of caring.

Some people do not identify themselves as carers. They often feel isolated and unable to ask for help. Others do not wish to be called 'carers', preferring to think of their role as wife or husband, son or daughter.

The work of carers is rarely broken down into the many separate services they offer. Families in particular often provide a full range of services for relatives with care needs. They carry out demanding tasks including nursing, bathing, dressing and lifting. Many help with very intimate caring tasks for people who are paralysed or who cannot move from their beds. Where people are suffering from mental illnesses, families must act as protectors and counsellors. Caring day after day can be exhausting and stressful – sometimes with little or no break – as well as rewarding.

The needs of carers are increasingly understood, mainly because of the work of the Carers National Association, an organisation of carers which has local groups all over the country. However, it can be easy not to offer services to someone with a carer on the grounds that they are already being helped and do not need more. This could mean that the carer has to stop caring before he or she really wishes to (see also p 86).

Of the 6.8 million carers identified in the 1990 survey, some 3.9 million – or 58 per cent – are women. In general, the survey found that women are more likely than men to take the main responsibility for caring for someone, and to spend 20 hours a week or more in caring. Women are also more likely than men to be involved in providing personal *and* physical care or mainly personal care, whereas men are more likely to provide just physical care or practical help.[6] It is argued that such differences arise partly because women are *expected* to take on a caring role, particularly for older relatives. In future, however, as the population ages and more women go out to work, it may be that fewer women will be willing or available to be carers. Population projections show that the number of women aged 45–64 (the peak age for caring) will not rise as fast as the number of very old people.

Carers may also be *users* of community care services, if they have care needs of their own, or if their caring tasks are such that they need help in supporting the person they care for. Carers often give up work, or work shorter hours, in order to be able to care.

The amount and kind of care provided by carers vary enormously, depending on the circumstances of the carer and the person needing care. Friends and neighbours are much less likely to provide a high level of personal care than are 'co-resident' carers – those who live with the person who needs care. Even when people live with someone, their 'network' of support may not be enough for their needs. Their carer may go to work or school, or may simply need extra help. Many families live far from their older relatives. Neighbours who once offered care may move away. 'Occasional' care may be relatively easy to arrange; but as needs increase, friends and relatives may be unable to provide enough.

### HOW MUCH FAMILY SUPPORT DO OLDER PEOPLE HAVE?

A high proportion of older people live away from their families. In 1992 in Britain 30 per cent of men and 50 per cent of women living at home and aged 75 or over lived alone. In 1987 61 per cent of women aged 80 or over living at home lived alone, with 21 per cent living with children or children-in-law, 11 per cent with their spouse and 7 per cent with other relatives or non-relatives.[7]

# 'Formal' care providers

Although most community care is in the 'informal' sector, the 'formal' sector provides essential support, through professionals and others who offer particular skills and kinds of care.

The formal sector has several different parts: the 'statutory' or 'public' sector; the 'voluntary' or 'charitable' sector; and the 'private' sector. Sometimes the private and voluntary sectors are lumped together and referred to as the 'independent' sector (see also p 106).

## The statutory sector

The statutory sector includes public authorities or bodies which have been created by law and which are paid for mainly through taxes. Statutory provision for community care comes mainly from the National Health Service and from local authorities, in particular the social services and housing departments. Local and health authorities are described in more detail later in this chapter.

Some services are 'directly' provided: the authority runs the services itself. Other services are 'indirectly' provided: the authority purchases them from some other organisation or authority. There are charges for many statutory services.

Workers in the statutory sector include community nurses, social workers and wardens of local authority retirement housing.

## The voluntary sector

The voluntary sector includes charities which provide services or represent particular interests. Voluntary or charitable organisations receive funding from many different sources, including charitable donations, sponsorship, grants from public bodies, and charges for some services. Voluntary sector organisations may provide some services through contracts with public authorities.

Some voluntary organisations are very specialised, for instance the Alzheimer's Disease Society, the National Schizophrenia Fellowship, or CancerLink. Each brings together people with particular conditions or problems, or their relatives. Members of local groups share years of experience and have often become expert in a particular type of care. Some groups may provide highly specialised services, staffed by paid workers or by highly trained volunteers. Other groups form self-help networks to support people with similar interests or needs.

Housing associations (see p 65) often specialise in provision for people with particular needs, such as young single homeless people or certain groups of older people.

It should be noted that the voluntary sector includes both paid and unpaid workers. 'Volunteers' – unpaid workers, or those who receive just an honorarium or expenses – work in all sectors, and continue to form the backbone of voluntary sector work. Many are former professional care workers; others have many years' experience in care work, and increasingly volunteers are trained to carry out complex caring and support work. However, the voluntary sector also makes extensive use of paid specialist workers.

## The private sector

The private sector includes companies or individuals offering a wide variety of services. The private sector raises money through its own trading activities – by selling goods or services. Private sector organisations may offer some services through contracts with the public sector. This sector provides a lot of residential and nursing home care – financed in part by public sector finance, through special rates of Income Support and local and health authority contracts – and some care for people at home.

The private sector includes large national corporations, which build and provide retirement housing and residential or nursing homes, and much smaller providers such as people who both own and manage care homes and small home care agencies. Local and health authorities will increasingly enter into contracts with private organisations to provide some of the care which they decide is necessary in their areas.

Not fitting into any of these categories are 'not-for-profit' organisations. Trusts have been formed, for instance, to take over the management of some local authority residential homes. (The word 'trust' in this context describes a form of not-for-profit organisation, as distinct from NHS trusts, described on p 31.)

# The local authority

There are several kinds of 'local authority', and people are not always sure who does what. At the time of writing, the system has been in place since local government reorganisation in 1974 (as modified in 1986). However, the Local Government Commission has undertaken a review of local authorities. As a result some counties will be divided into smaller 'unitary' authorities responsible for all local services. In other areas, some cities will become unitary authorities, leaving the rest of the county intact.

At present, who does what in England depends on whether you live in a county or a metropolitan or London borough. A person in a county has *two* 'local authorities': the county council and the district (or borough) council. Examples of counties are Northumberland and Cornwall. Districts within those counties are Alnwick and Penwith. Examples of metropolitan boroughs are Tameside and Sandwell. Southwark is a London borough.

**County councils** are responsible for social services, some education and a range of other services. Counties can be quite large. The work of their social services departments is usually broken down to cover local areas. Other activities, such as planning, may also be 'devolved' to these local areas. Each authority has its own pattern of working.

**District (or borough) councils** usually cover a town or several towns. They are responsible for housing, leisure services, environmental health, and a variety of other services. In some areas, district councils have taken responsibility for some social services, such as day care.

**Metropolitan or London boroughs** are unitary authorities. This means that there is just one 'local authority' or council. It runs social services, housing, education, and all the other services mentioned above.

The new 'unitary' authorities will have similar functions to the above. It is possible that some unitary authorities may be too small to carry out all functions on their own, and that for some services larger groupings of authorities may be needed.

Each type of local authority has an elected council which decides within its legal responsibilities how much of which kinds of services the authority will provide. Officers of the various departments are respon-sible for carrying out the policies of elected members of the council, and for advising them about policy choices. All the activities of the local authority – which is a 'statutory authority' – are carried out through the authority of various Acts of Parliament. These Acts create duties – things the local authority *must* do – and powers – things the local authority *may* do (see p 52). Some Acts which cover community care services are described in Appendix 2.

# Health authorities

The NHS Executive has been set up by the Government as part of the Department of Health to run the NHS. There are currently three kinds of health authority: the Regional Health Authority, the District Health Authority and the Family Health Services Authority (formerly the Family Practitioner Committee). The National Health Service has been reformed following the 1989 White Paper *Working for Patients*. New systems of arranging services have been introduced and NHS trusts have been created which provide NHS services but are not under direct control of the District Health Authority. Many general practitioners (referred to as GP fundholders) have taken on new responsibilities for purchasing services in place of those formerly carried out by the District Health Authority.

## Regional Health Authorities

The Regional Health Authority (RHA) is currently responsible for overseeing the activities of District Health Authorities (DHAs) and Family Health Services Authorities (FHSAs). RHAs are at present the link between the National Health Service Executive and the DHAs and FHSAs. RHAs may advise DHAs and FHSAs about what they expect to see in local plans for health services.

## District Health Authorities

The DHA is responsible for assessing the health needs of its resident population and arranging care to meet these needs, within the limits of available resources. The DHA can purchase this care from providers, which may include NHS trusts, the few remaining units directly managed by the DHA, or private or voluntary providers. By April 1995, 98 per cent of NHS hospital and community health services will be run by NHS trusts.[8] In some areas the purchasing function of several authorities may be brought together in 'purchasing consortia', or 'commissions'.

## Family Health Services Authorities

The FHSA (formerly the Family Practitioner Committee) is responsible for GPs, dentists, opticians and pharmacists working in the community. The FHSA works with the DHA to assess the health needs of the local population. It has some powers to allocate people to a GP's list, if the person is unable to find a GP. In 1996 it is planned to merge DHAs and FHSAs.

---

### THE HEALTH AUTHORITIES BILL

At the time of writing, the Health Authorities Bill was being debated in Parliament. It aims in April 1996 to:

■ abolish Regional Health Authorities, which will be replaced by regional outposts of the National Health Service Executive (in anticipation of this change, England's health regions were reduced to eight in number in April 1994. These eight regions will form the new Executive outposts from April 1996, if the legislation is passed);

■ create new health authorities, by merging District Health Authorities and Family Health Services Authorities, to create a 'single authority responsible for ensuring that the entire health needs of their populations are met . . . to ensure that the hospital, the community and the family doctor services are planned together in a coherent and co-ordinated way'.[9] (In anticipation of the move to unified health authorities, some DHAs and FHSAs have 'joint commissioning' arrangements, whereby they work in close cooperation; in some areas the authorities have appointed a single chief executive, but the pattern differs from area to area.)

The Government's aims in these changes are to:

■ reduce bureaucracy and continue the devolution of responsibility for health services to the local level;

■ make savings in administrative costs (although there is debate about the extent of savings which will result);

■ move towards more influence for family doctors, with expectations that the new health authorities will work 'especially closely with the family doctors in their areas – fundholders and non-fundholders alike'.[10] This is part of the Government's aim to move 'towards a primary care-led NHS' (see EL (94) 79 *Developing NHS purchasing and GP fundholding*).

---

The NHS is thus continuing to evolve from the reforms begun in 1989. Many of the changes in funding, administration and responsibility have a direct impact on community care.

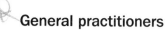

## General practitioners

General practitioners are organised in two different ways. The NHS reforms created 'general practitioner (or GP) fundholders'. These fundholding practices administer their own budgets: they are responsible for purchasing certain types of health care for their patients, including some non-emergency inpatient care, a range of outpatient services, community mental health services and community nursing, and care for individual patients costing up to £6,000 per year. Fundholders pay for practice staff costs and the costs of medicines for their patients.

The Government has actively promoted the move to GP fundholding, suggesting that patients receive better, more responsive care. In October 1994, the Secretary of State for Health announced that the fundholding scheme will be expanded to include more practices than had previously been eligible. Preparations will begin from April 1995 and the scheme is planned to be fully operational from April 1996. The minimum practice size for fundholders in England will be reduced from 7,000 to 5,000, and the scope of the scheme will be extended to include, among other things, virtually all elective surgery and outpatients and specialist nursing services. Smaller practices with 3,000 to 5,000 patients will be able to become 'community' fundholders, with budgets to cover diagnostic tests, staff, and most of the community services in the standard scheme, but not acute hospital care or outpatient services.

In addition, various pilot schemes are being established where around 50 practices are able to purchase the full range of hospital and community health services, including accident and emergency.[11] It is expected that the different 'pilot' schemes will be fully evaluated.

The Government has made extra funds available to GPs who become fundholders, but the extent to which the scheme will expand is not clear. By April 1995 it is estimated that there will be around 2,500 fundholding practices, covering about 40 per cent of the population.[12]

Some general practitioners do not wish to join the scheme, arguing that non-fundholders can become efficient and effective purchasers for their patients (using services purchased by the District Health Authority) and avoid the management costs of setting up fundholding practices. There is now a National Association of Commissioning GPs alongside the National Association of Fundholding General Practices.

The growth of fundholding affects planning within the NHS, and therefore for community care. The *Working for Patients* reforms set up a purchaser–provider split (discussed more fully on pp 107–108). This means that health authorities plan for the needs of their local populations and purchase services from providers, as described above. Yet fundholding GPs are independently contracted to provide services to the NHS. As fundholding grows – and as funds are diverted from DHAs to the fundholder scheme – so the ability of the DHA to plan and purchase services for local populations is diminished. The single health authorities proposed for 1996 will bring together DHAs and FHSAs, but this will not of itself resolve the issue of the overlapping planning and purchasing responsibilities of health authorities and fundholding GPs. This issue is set to be the subject of more discussion and debate in the future.

## Community Health Councils

The Community Health Council (CHC) is not a health 'authority'. It acts as a kind of consumer watchdog for local health services, representing the views of users to the relevant health authorities. It gives information and advice to the public about problems with local health services, and tells people how to make a complaint.

## Working with local authorities

Despite the fact that they often have different boundaries, health and local authorities are expected to work together in planning for community care. However, health authorities are run quite differently from local authorities. Their members are not elected. They are appointed by authority of central government. Cooperation in planning is discussed on pages 66–71.

---

This chapter has looked at who might need community care, and who might provide it. By describing current changes, it gives a hint as to the complexity of community care provision. The rest of the book is about the NHS and Community Care Act and the White Paper *Caring for People*. The next chapter looks briefly at the history of community care and at events leading up to the Act. The following six chapters describe the major areas of change which have been introduced since the Act was passed in 1990.

# 2 The Development of Community Care

Before looking at the reforms we should look briefly at the development of community care. History reminds us that there is no 'right' solution to achieving good community care. In all probability the current changes will eventually become just another part of a long quest for an elusive ideal.

Several themes have dominated thinking about community care for nearly 40 years. Although the *ideal* of community care is broadly supported by everyone, the *practice* has varied and has often been found to be deficient.

Themes of the *ideal* include:

- the belief that people would rather be cared for in their own homes, or in small homelike places;

- the belief that it is better to care for people out of large institutions, fuelled by evidence that large institutions cannot offer personalised, stimulating environments for either residents or staff;

- a belief in the worth and dignity of each person needing care;

- the belief that reorganisation of services, authorities and professional ways of working will improve services.

Themes of the *practice* include:

- a concern with the high cost of care in institutions, and a belief that care at home is cheaper;

- a difficulty on the part of different authorities and organisations in working constructively together to improve services;

- the struggle to give priority to care for people with chronic illness or disabling conditions;
- competition between client groups when resources are stretched;
- a conflict between the belief that services are most appropriately planned and provided at local level and the need, as seen by successive governments, to reduce or tightly control public expenditure;
- a gradual change in the philosophy of public services from 'universal' provision, available as of right and according to need, to 'selective' provision, dependent on means and limited to those in greatest need;
- a change in the philosophy of public social provision to a 'mixed economy', with more emphasis on the private and voluntary sectors as providers;
- a move from support for collective – or state – provision to a belief that individuals should take increasing responsibility for themselves.

# THE PROBLEM OF INSTITUTIONALISATION

During the nineteenth century large institutions were built for people with mental illness or mental handicap. People became 'institutionalised' in these hospitals, less able to cope with normal life and dependent on the routine and narrow confines of long-stay institutions.

During the 1950s the nature of such 'institutionalisation' became better understood. The effects of certain mental illnesses could be controlled by new drugs, without the need for hospital treatment. In 1957 a Royal Commission report on the law relating to mental illness stated that the time had come for a shift from hospital care to community care. It recommended a 'general reorientation away from institutional care in its present form and towards community care'.

Further evidence about the effects of institutionalisation was collected during the 1960s. In 1962, Peter Townsend surveyed local authority, private and voluntary residential homes. In *The Last Refuge*, he reported that many people in such homes were there not because they needed care, but for other social reasons: homelessness, insufficient home care, lack of resources, or no family to care for them. He found that conditions in homes reduced the autonomy of the residents and isolated them. In 1969, Pauline Morris, in her book *Put Away*, looked at 'mental subnormality' hospitals. Once again, she found little need for people to be in hospitals, which were isolated and poorly staffed.

In 1969 an inquiry at Ely Hospital investigated the first in a series of scandals involving bad practice in large institutions. This report and others led in the early 1970s to Government White Papers proposing improvements in services for people with mental illness and mental handicap. (A White Paper is an official Government document setting out what the Government proposes to do about a particular issue. It normally leads to a law to bring the changes about.) These documents focused on the need to find ways of enabling people to be cared for in their own homes – or at least out of large institutions. They called for improved coordination of services, and for much more support for people in their own homes. The same arguments are still being put forward today.

## The first community care plans

In 1962, an ambitious hospital plan[13] stated that large mental illness hospitals should gradually be closed and that local authorities should develop more services for people in their own homes and in residential homes. In 1963 local authorities were asked to report on the expected needs of their populations, and their current provision of health and welfare services. Responses to this request[14] were called the first community care plans, although they differed considerably from the plans we will discuss in Chapter 3. They showed great variations in the provision of services between local authorities in similar areas.

Already, then, some themes were in place: concern about the effects of large institutions, and a realisation that local services varied enormously.

# HEALTH AND LOCAL GOVERNMENT REORGANISATIONS

During the 1970s, there was an increasing emphasis on improving the *structures* of authorities and organisations. In 1970, the Local Authority Social Services Act created social services departments as we now know them. The Act took effect in 1972. The idea of setting up social services departments had arisen from a concern about welfare services for children. A committee was set up to look at how social services could be arranged in order to develop an effective *family* service. The Seebohm Report, produced in 1968, then extended the definition of 'the family' beyond the focus on children:

> We could only make sense of our task by considering also childless couples and individuals without any close relatives: in other words, everybody.[15]

The Seebohm Report proposed that personal social services should be brought together into one department, the social services department. This would serve as a single source of help in each local authority for anyone with social care needs. Social workers who had previously specialised in working with children, or with blind people, for instance, were to become 'generic' workers – able to deal with all types of problem.

This reorganisation of social services brought together many 'welfare' services, but during this period some of the services that local authorities had traditionally run were transferred to the National Health Service. These included home nursing, a service of crucial importance in today's community care arrangements. Sorting out 'social services' provision thus brought about a firmer split between 'health' and 'welfare' functions. Since then, a major theme of community care policies has been the need for improved coordination between health and social services.

The National Health Service was given a new structure in 1974, with revisions in 1982. In 1974 hospital social workers were moved from health authorities to social services. In 1974 local government was also reorganised, and some areas now face reorganisation again (see p 30).

Each of these changes aimed to create *structures* through which better services could be provided. They were based on current thinking about ideal sizes of authorities and good working practice. Such changes almost always represent some compromise between Government, administrators, professionals and local politicians and populations; in time, they yield to new changes based on different thinking.

The great changes in health and social services during the 1970s took place in the climate of optimism created by a new Act of Parliament, the Chronically Sick and Disabled Persons (CSDP) Act.

## The Chronically Sick and Disabled Persons Act 1970

The CSDP Act required local authorities to find out the needs of people in their local populations and to provide certain services for them. These services had to be publicised.

The CSDP Act is still in force today. It has been strengthened by the Disabled Persons (Services, Consultation and Representation) Act 1986. However, then as now, local authorities varied greatly in how they responded to the Act. (Both Acts are described more fully in Chapter 4 (pp 79–80); Appendix 1 describes the provisions of the 1986 Act.)

The hopes which the Act had stimulated gradually gave way to caution about what could be achieved. During the 1970s economic pressures meant that the Government of the day restricted public spending by local authorities – even if this meant that they could not fulfil all their duties under various Acts of Parliament.

# COMPETING PRIORITIES

## Acute and non-acute services

Other pressures affected progress in community care. There was competition for resources in the health service, particularly between acute and non-acute services. Most community care health needs are chronic needs: many people require continuing supervision or nursing care; many suffer from progressive diseases, such as Parkinson's disease or Alzheimer's disease. Many others face problems because of arthritis or rheumatism or the effects of stroke or permanent disablement.

These conditions are not 'glamorous', and it is often argued that they do badly in the competition for resources with acute services. New technology has created wonderful possibilities for treatment, but it has also brought much higher health-care costs. Sometimes the gains have been at the expense of improved services for people with less dramatic needs, which are, however, no less painful or traumatic in their effects.

## Different client groups

At about the same time as the hospital scandals, child care also created headlines. The Maria Colwell case in 1974 was followed by a series of child abuse cases which forced social services departments to review their practices with regard to children at risk. Many departments, facing cutbacks in finance, had to reduce their services for other people, particularly bearing in mind that child care services are largely 'mandatory' – they must be provided – while many adult services are not.

These conflicting pressures continue. The 1989 Children Act has placed new responsibilities on social services departments, and some are hard pressed to find the staff and money to meet these new responsibilities, at the same time as improving their support for adults with a wide range of care needs.

## More people needing care

Growing numbers of people live in the community and need care. Changes in the structure of the population have meant that striving to improve community care services often seems like running hard just to stand still. In 1941 only 10 per cent of the population was aged 65 or over, compared with 15.8 per cent today.

**DEMOGRAPHY**

The study of populations is called demography. One example of demographic change is the increase in the numbers of people aged over 80 or over 85, or the increase in the proportion of such people compared with the rest of the population. Demography is important in planning for all types of services.

Life expectancy at birth was 48 years for males and 51.6 years for females born in 1906; 58.4 years for males and 62.4 years for females born in 1931; and 66.2 years for males and 71.2 years for females born in 1951. At the same time, the life expectancy remaining to people who have grown old has also increased. In 1906, a man reaching the age of 60 could expect to live another 13.4 years on average; a woman, 14.9 years. In 1991, a man reaching the age of 60 could expect to live another 17.8 years, and a woman, 21.8 years.[16]

The numbers of older people have thus grown enormously, and the 'survivors' of earlier years are now living to a very old age. Between 1993 and 2003, the numbers of people aged 85 or over will grow from 963,000 to nearly 1.2 million. Although old age is not a disease, the increase in the ageing population does create more demand for services. So do changes in other groups who need care and support. Where long-stay hospitals have closed, for instance, people have been resettled and require services in the community. Children with learning disabilities are no longer sent to hospital for life – they and their families require support in the community. People with HIV and AIDS form a new group of people needing support, and there is a growing awareness of the needs of older people in this group and of older family members and carers.

# CONCERN WITH THE COST OF COMMUNITY CARE

The growth in the numbers of older people has been accompanied by a change in the method of financing long-term care. From 1980 special social security help with paying for care in residential and nursing homes was available to anyone who qualified on grounds of income and savings, with no assessment of the person's need for a particular type of care. This help was given through special rates of Supplementary Benefit, and then Income Support. It was this system which changed in April 1993, and which has been at the root of the community care reforms.

In the early 1980s, the benefit was payable according to local limits set by local offices of the Department of Health and Social Security, as it was then called. This led to enormous differences in the amount of benefit paid in different areas, and was considered to be open to abuse. It was said that it led to unnecessarily high fees being charged by some homes. The system was changed in 1985 to a system of national limits for different types of care home and different categories of care.

The effects of this system began to cause concern in the mid-1980s, when attention focused both on the increasing cost of residential and nursing home care and on the problems of shifting the balance of care from long-term hospital or residential provision to other types of care.

# The 1986 Audit Commission report

In 1981 the Department of Health and Social Security published *Report of a Study on Community Care* which reviewed in some detail the themes we have discussed in this chapter. This report found that there had been 'little identifiable shift in the balance of care for those elderly people on the margin between institutional and community-based care', stressed the importance of close collaboration between health and social services authorities, and noted that ways must be found to shift the balance of resources between the NHS and social services. Following that report, a consultative document was published suggesting how this might be done, but in practice the social security system described above began to affect the distribution of funds for care.

The Audit Commission, an organisation which monitors local government and health expenditure, produced a major report on the subject in 1986.

*Making a Reality of Community Care* suggested that the availability of Supplementary Benefit payments for residential and nursing home care was 'skewing' public expenditure for people with care needs. It was too easy for people to go into homes with public support, and this was discouraging the development of effective services for people in their own homes.

Furthermore, the report said, it would cost less in many cases to help people to remain at home, thus reflecting the belief that it is cheaper to help people remain in their own homes than to keep them in institutions.

A warning note on this belief had, however, been sounded in the 1981 report mentioned above:

> For some people community-based packages of care may not always be a less expensive or more effective alternative to residential or hospital provision, particularly for those living alone. In some cases the community alternative might only appear cheap because its level of provision could be considered inadequate.                    *Report of a Study on Community Care*, para 3.27

This statement could equally well be made today, and appears increasingly relevant as local authorities struggle to balance the costs of care for people at home compared with costs in a care home (see p 94).

# The Griffiths Report

Following the Audit Commission report, the Government asked Sir Roy Griffiths to look at the organisation and funding of community care services. The Griffiths Report – *Community Care: Agenda for action* – became the baseline for the changes described in the 1989 White Paper *Caring for People* and in the NHS and Community Care Act 1990.

Griffiths was asked

> to review the way in which public funds are used to support community care policy and to advise . . . on the options for action that would improve the use of these funds as a contribution to more effective community care.
>
> Griffiths Report, p iii, para 2

He said that his report identified 'roadblocks' to the effective planning and delivery of community care services. He proposed that a Minister of State should be 'clearly identified as being responsible for community care' (para 6.19). Social services managers should aim to ensure that 'the right services are provided in good time, to the people who need them most' (p 28).

Griffiths said that people should be helped 'to stay in their own homes for as long as possible, or in as near a domestic environment as possible, so that residential, nursing home and hospital care is reserved for those whose needs cannot be met in any other way' (p 28).

In order to do this, he said that social services authorities must:

(i) have systems which enable them to identify those who have need of care and support in the community;

(ii) assess those needs within the context of the individual's own situation;

(iii) taking account of the views and wishes of the person to be cared for, and any informal carers, decide what packages of care would be best suited to the needs, whether provided directly or indirectly;

(iv) determine the priority to be given to the case, given the total resources available and the competing needs of others;

(v) arrange delivery of the services decided upon;

(vi) keep under review the delivery of that package of services, and the individual's needs and circumstances.  para 3.8

Griffiths proposed that money from central government be specially reserved for local authorities to spend on community care. This would include some money taken from the social security budget, in place of the special benefit for residential and nursing home care. (Reserving money to be spent for a particular purpose is sometimes referred to as 'ring-fencing'.)

People who are able to should pay the full economic cost of services provided in their own homes. People should also be encouraged to plan ahead to meet their own care needs. 'Encouraging those who can afford to plan ahead to do so should help to ensure that public resources are concentrated on those in greatest need' (para 6.62).

Griffiths proposed that local authorities should be required to draw up plans showing how they would cooperate with health and housing authorities to provide services which are broadly in line with Government policy. Services should be provided according to the needs and wishes of individuals and their carers. 'The people receiving help will have a greater say in what is done to help them, and a wider choice' (p 28). The local authority should be the 'lead authority' for this, as it is the democratically elected authority closest to service users.

Griffiths noted the importance of general practitioners, community nurses and other health workers in community care, and suggested the creation of a new kind of worker, a 'community carer' (para 8.4) to break down some of the barriers between health and social care (see p 70).

Although traditionally welfare services are provided mainly by the local authority, Griffiths said that such monopoly provision is not necessarily in the interests of service users: the local authority should become an 'enabler' – acting as the 'designers, organisers and purchasers of non-health care services' (para 1.3.4) and not as monopolistic providers.

Before going on to look at the White Paper *Caring for People*, which incorporated many of Griffiths' recommendations, we should mention the publication of the influential Wagner Report on residential care (see box). Whereas Griffiths had been asked to look at the organisation and funding of care services, Wagner focused on issues of quality and choice – the ideals of community care. Her report, too, contributed to the ideas contained in the White Paper.

## THE WAGNER REPORT

Within a week of the publication of Griffiths' report in 1988, another very important report was published by a committee chaired by Gillian Wagner: *Residential Care: A positive choice.*

The Wagner Report emphasises the positive role of residential care, and the scope for positive choices to be made by residents both on entering such care and while they are in it. Needs for **care** should be separated from needs for **accommodation**: people should not have to move just because their care needs change.

Local authorities should play a lead role in planning accommodation and support services. A statutory duty should be placed on local authorities to propose to individuals a reasonable package of services to enable them to remain at home if that is their choice and it is reasonable to do so.

The report emphasises the rights of the individual as a citizen. Residents of residential homes should have:

*a trial period of residence; an agreed contract; access to community services and facilities; privacy; management of their own financial affairs where feasible; access to formalised complaints procedures, supported where appropriate by an advocate or representative.*

Staff should have adequate training; all homes should be inspected, including those run by the local authority; and the Government should consider bringing nursing homes and residential homes under the same registration and inspection rules.

The Wagner Report's 'five Cs' brought together the principles or values which should form the basis of good practice:

**Caring**
*This should be personal, and residents should feel valued, safe and secure.*

**Choice**
*Each resident's right to exercise choice over their daily life should be respected.*

**Continuity**
*This includes both consistency of care from staff, and the maintenance of links with a resident's previous life.*

**Change**
*For residents, the opportunity for continued development; for staff, a commitment to respond to changing needs.*

**Common values**
*Ensuring that practice is based on a shared philosophy and values.*

Wagner Report, p 60

# THE WHITE PAPER
## *CARING FOR PEOPLE*

It took the Government about 20 months to prepare its response to Griffiths' and Wagner's reports. The White Paper *Caring for People* was published in November 1989. It set out the framework for the community care reforms which the rest of this book is about.

Many – though not all – of Griffiths' and Wagner's recommendations found their way into the White Paper. The Government agreed that the special social security allowances for residential and nursing home care should end, and that the money this would have cost should be given to local authorities to make arrangements for care. But the money should not be 'ring-fenced', as it was thought to be better for local authorities to make their own decisions about how to spend their money. (In fact some of the transferred money has been ring-fenced. This is called the Special Transitional Grant and is described on pp 165–167.)

The Government did not accept the idea of a duty on local authorities to propose 'reasonable' packages of care, as recommended by the Wagner Report. Nor did it accept the need to move towards a unified system of inspection for residential and nursing homes.

The White Paper outlined six *key objectives* and seven *key changes* needed to bring about the objectives. The objectives are described in para 1.11 of the document. We will look at each of them in turn.

## The six key objectives
### Services for people at home

1 **'To promote the development of domiciliary, day and respite services to enable people to live in their own homes wherever feasible and sensible . . . In future the Government will encourage the targeting of home-based services on those people whose need for them is greatest.'**

Domiciliary, day and respite services are the three key types of services which should help people to stay at home. *Domiciliary* means 'home-based': domiciliary services would include home help or home care, occupational therapy, and perhaps bathing services. *Day* services include all the different types of daytime care outside a person's home – such as a day centre, luncheon club or day hospital. *Respite* services allow carers and people being cared for to have a break from each other (see box).

---

**RESPITE CARE**

A 'respite' means a break. Carers in particular need regular respite, so that they can have time off from caring to pursue their own interests. Respite is also important for the person being cared for, who may welcome a break from being looked after by the same person all the time.

A respite break might be arranged in a person's own home: someone comes in while the carer goes out. Or it could be arranged in a residential home, nursing home or hospital – for instance if the carer goes away on holiday. Some respite care is provided in other people's homes and day centres. Carers need to know that respite care is available in an emergency, say if they become ill.

---

This first objective includes the idea of 'targeting'. In the past, it was sometimes said that services were spread too thinly: a lot of people whose needs were not particularly great may have received very little of a service, say an hour or two of home help per week. The Government now aims to make best use of resources by encouraging local authorities to 'target' services on the people with the greatest needs. In some areas, this means that home help, for instance, is no longer provided. 'Home care' services are being 'targeted' on people who have care needs as well as a need for help with housework. If people only require help with housework, they may no longer receive a service from the local authority.

## Services for carers

2   **'To ensure that service providers make practical support for carers a high priority.'**

We have already seen that carers – family, neighbours, friends – provide most community care. Such people need recognition and support in order to continue caring. Many need financial help, and consideration of their own needs when assessments for care are being made. They need information about services, and regular, reliable support. (See also p 86.)

## Assessments for care

3 'To make proper assessment of need and good case management the cornerstone of high quality care. Packages of care should then be designed in line with individual needs and preferences.'

A major concern leading to the Griffiths Report was the use of large sums of public money for residential and nursing home care, without proper assessment of need. It has been argued that many people receiving such care might not need it if appropriate services were available in the community. In addition, it has often been said that services provided to people with care needs are picked 'off the shelf' – chosen from what is available, rather than being offered in relation to what the person needs.

A further problem with assessment was that many different people carried out assessments. A home care organiser would assess for home care; an occupational therapist would assess for aids within the home; a nurse would assess for the bathing service, and so on. The White Paper aimed to reduce unnecessary duplication and to bring better coordination to complex assessments through the social services department.

## A 'mixed economy of care'

4 'To promote the development of a flourishing independent sector alongside good quality public services . . . social services authorities should be "enabling" agencies. It is their responsibility to make maximum possible use of private and voluntary providers.'

The Government believes that a variety of providers will increase choice for service users, and that better services will result from increased competition. Local authorities' community care plans (see Chapter 3) must show how they will encourage independent sector providers. This policy is in line with the Government's aim of reducing the level of public services, and has been reinforced by Government restrictions on spending the Special Transitional Grant (see pp 165–167).

In areas where there has been a long-standing tradition of strong public services, some authorities have been reluctant to encourage provision by other sectors. There may also be areas where the private and voluntary sectors do not wish to develop. There is, for instance, little independent sector residential and nursing home care in some inner city areas. This means that the 'mixed economy of care' looks very different in different local authorities.

## A clear demarcation of responsibilities

5 **'To clarify the responsibilities of agencies and so make it easier to hold them to account for their performance.'**

One aim of the White Paper was to make sure that people knew who was responsible for which services. Community care plans should show who will do what. There may be confusion, however, about the division of responsibility between health and local authorities for people with health and social care needs. The White Paper states that health authorities' responsibilities remain unchanged under the new community care arrangements – yet local authorities have had responsibilities since April 1993 to assess people who need support from public funds for places in nursing homes, as well as in residential homes. This has led to negotiation between health and local authorities as to who is responsible for the continuing care of certain people, a subject we discuss more fully on pages 172–174. Local and health authorities have to sort out their respective responsibilities for continuing nursing care in order to qualify to receive the money to be transferred from the social security budget. Such arrangements have not always reflected patients' rights (see pp 173–174).

## Better value for taxpayers' money

6 **'To secure better value for taxpayers' money by introducing a new funding structure for social care . . . social security provisions should not . . . provide any incentive in favour of residential and nursing home care.'**

The transfer of Department of Social Security money to local authorities is meant to remove the incentive which previously existed for both health and local authorities to place people in care homes, where they could claim benefit from the Department of Social Security. The issues which this raises are discussed in Chapter 8.

# Key changes

To carry out these objectives, the White Paper (para 1.12) proposed the following key changes:

1 'Local authorities will be responsible, in collaboration with medical, nursing and other interests, for assessing individual need, designing care arrangements, and securing their delivery within available resources.' (See Chapter 4 on assessment and care management.)

2 'Local authorities will be expected to produce and publish clear plans for the development of community care services, consistent with the plans of health authorities and other interested agencies.' (See Chapter 3 on community care plans.)

3 'Local authorities will be expected to show that they are making maximum use of the independent sector.' (See Chapters 3 and 5 on community care plans and on purchasing and contracting.)

4 'There will be a new funding structure for those seeking public support for residential and nursing home care from April [1993]. After that date local authorities will take responsibility for financial support of people in private and voluntary homes, over and above general social security entitlements. The new arrangements will not, however, apply to people already resident in homes before April [1993]', who will continue under the existing system. (See Chapter 8 on paying for care.)

5 'Applicants with few or no resources of their own will be eligible for the same levels of Income Support and Housing Benefit, irrespective of whether they are living in their own homes or in independent residential or nursing homes.'

People who have entered private and voluntary care homes since 1 April 1993 have had access to a new residential allowance paid as part of Income Support (rather than Housing Benefit, as referred to in the White Paper). The new allowance is explained on page 158.

The Government has deliberately withheld support for housing costs through the residential allowance from people in homes directly run by the local authority: it wants local authorities to encourage independent sector care homes, and has thus ensured that the local authority will pay more from its own funds for people cared for in its own homes.

6 'Local authorities will be required to establish inspection and registration at arms-length from the management of their own services which is

responsible for checking on standards in both their own homes and in independent sector residential care homes.'

The Government accepted the Wagner Report's recommendations that local authority homes should be inspected, but rejected the recommendation that new independent inspectorates should be responsible for both residential and nursing homes. The responsibility for inspecting all residential homes therefore rests with the local authority, but inspection must be separate – at 'arms-length' – from the authority's management of its own homes. (See Chapter 7 on inspection.)

7 'There will be a new specific grant to promote the development of social care for seriously mentally ill people.'

The Government recognised that social services expenditure for people with mental health problems was often only a small part of a local authority's budget. It therefore proposed to create a separate special grant which, unlike most local authority money for community care, would be 'ring-fenced' specially for projects for people with mental health problems. Local authorities must add some money of their own to the grant, and must agree on the projects with their local health authorities. Similar grants are available for services for people with HIV/AIDS and those who misuse drugs and alcohol, for social services training, and (for children) for guardians ad litem and reporting officers.

The White Paper also proposed that local authority social services departments should set up new complaints procedures (see Chapter 6).

At first, the Government proposed that the community care reforms should all take place by April 1991. This allowed very little time between the publication of the White Paper and full implementation of the reforms. An Act of Parliament was needed to make the necessary changes in the law – in addition to those needed for the reorganisation of the National Health Service, which was taking place at the same time. The NHS and Community Care Act became law in June 1990. In July 1990, the Government announced that the changes would not take place all at once. They would be phased in between 1991 and 1993.

# The NHS and Community Care Act 1990

Changes in the law were necessary for some of the recommendations in the White Paper. These included:

- amending the National Assistance Act 1948, to allow local authorities to make arrangements for people to be cared for in nursing homes, as well as in residential homes (section 42 and the Community Care (Residential Accommodation) Act 1992, which replaces section 42(2) of the 1990 Act);

- creating a duty for local authorities to prepare community care plans in consultation with health and housing authorities, and with certain voluntary organisations (section 46);

- creating a duty (in addition to their existing duty to assess under the Disabled Persons Act 1986) for local authorities to assess people who may be in need of community care services and to decide whether these needs call for provision by them of such services (section 47);

- creating an additional power for local authorities to inspect their own residential homes, and other community care services provided or arranged by them (section 48);

- giving the Secretary of State powers to direct local authorities to carry out certain social services tasks, including the setting up of complaints procedures and the provision of new grants for mental illness and drug and alcohol problems; and giving 'default powers' to the Secretary of State to order a local authority to carry out certain duties, if it has failed to carry out these duties with respect to social services (section 50).

## POWERS AND DUTIES

Local authorities have powers and duties. A *power* is something they are able to do, but do not have to. They have the power, for instance, to provide recreation and leisure services. However, they have a duty to provide certain social services – for instance, they must provide residential care for people who need it and for whom it is not otherwise available (under the National Assistance Act 1948); and certain social services for disabled people (under the Chronically Sick and Disabled Persons Act 1970).

There are no set amounts of the services which authorities must provide under these statutory duties. Each case must be judged individually.

The Government has issued guidance to local authorities about carrying out the community care reforms. The Policy Guidance (*Community Care in the Next Decade and Beyond*) tells local and health authorities what is expected of them if they are to meet the Government's proposals on community care. The Policy Guidance covers all aspects of the community care reforms. There have been revisions to the section on inspection (see Chapter 7).

Practice Guidance has also been issued by the Department of Health on most aspects of the changes. It covers in much more detail what local authorities might do in carrying out each part of the changes.

The idea of community care is not new. Different *ideals* of community care have been pursued for nearly 40 years. Themes of these years have included concern about quality and availability of care, coupled with a desire to get the 'system' right, to develop the roles of professional workers, and to limit public spending. The aim of developing community care for people at home has been rooted in the belief that such care is preferable for and desired by most people. It has been believed (but not confirmed) to be cheaper than care in institutions.

The rest of this book looks at the main changes which have been introduced as part of the community care reforms. It looks in more detail at the White Paper, the 1990 Act and the Government's Policy and Practice Guidance. It comments on developments in the reformed system in its first 21 months.

# 3 Community Care Plans

Planning is – or should be – the activity which underpins most work. Yet it is easy to pass over in a hurry. Too often we are impatient to get on with the job, thinking it a waste of time to stop to make a plan – to set aims and objectives; to consider what resources we have and how we can best use them; to check on what we are doing, revising our plans in the light of the information we receive.

The community care reforms recognised this reluctance by creating a duty in law for local authorities to prepare community care plans. This chapter sets out what the 1990 Act said about plans, looks at the Government's guidance to local authorities, and considers recent developments in the planning process. These include continuing concern about the boundaries between health and social care; and development of the theme of 'planning' from an exercise of taking stock and setting targets to the additional tasks of 'managing the market' in ways which help independent sector providers to expand and develop their work.

## HOW SHOULD THE PLANS BE DRAWN UP?

### The White Paper and the Act

The White Paper *Caring for People* said that local authorities must prepare community care plans, which should state objectives and priorities for community care, and set specific targets for meeting these. The plans must be made public, and must link with the community care plans of other authorities – the housing department, the District Health Authority and the Family Health Services Authority.

---

**WHAT THE 1990 NHS AND COMMUNITY CARE ACT AND
GOVERNMENT DIRECTIONS SAY ABOUT PLANNING**

Section 46 states that local authorities must follow the directions of the Secretary of State to prepare and publish a community care plan, keep the plan under review, and change it or produce a new one if they are directed to do so by the Secretary of State. They must consult any District Health Authority and Family Health Services Authority which is in their area. If they are not a housing authority, they must consult the housing authority, if the plan may affect or be affected by the provision or availability of housing. They must also consult voluntary housing agencies, and voluntary organisations which represent users of services or their carers.

The Government has issued two Directions on community care planning, which have the force of law. In early 1993, a Direction stated that the planning process must include consultation with representatives of independent service providers. In 1994, a Direction required local authorities to include in their first plans after June 1994 their proposals for making arrangements to purchase independent sector non-residential community care services. These Directions reflect the Government's desire to move towards a 'mixed economy of care'; they also constitute its response to concerns on the part of the independent sector about their involvement in community care planning (see p 63).

---

The local authority – the county, metropolitan borough or London borough – is the 'lead authority' in community care planning. It should bring together all the main service purchasers and service providers and produce an agreed plan, showing who will do what.

Health authorities are also expected to prepare plans showing their community care policies. They can do this by themselves, or as part of the local authority community care plan. Many plans are jointly produced and signed by health and social services authorities, sometimes including housing as well.

The Government's Policy Guidance describes how local and health authorities should tackle the planning task. It gives guidance on how different authorities should cooperate with each other in preparing plans. As shown below, Government guidance on planning has changed each year, to reflect experience both in planning and in the overall implementation of the community care reforms.

# WHAT SHOULD THE PLANS CONTAIN?

The following is a summary from the Policy Guidance (para 2.25) of what social services departments should have shown in their first community care plans in 1992:

- a summary of the needs of the local population and the client groups for whom they intended to arrange services;

- a description of existing services, how priorities would be chosen, how social services departments intended to offer practical help, such as respite care, to carers, and how they planned to develop services for people at home;

- how quality in providing and purchasing services would be ensured and checked on (and what part inspection units and complaints procedures would play in this);

- how they intended to increase consumer choice and stimulate the development of a mixed economy of care;

- how much their plans would cost, what staff would be needed, and how money and staff would be used most effectively;

- how the authority had consulted with others in preparing plans;

- how it planned to tell service users and carers about services, and when the next plan would be published.

The plans were also to describe how other aspects of the community care reforms would be carried out – how inspection units and complaints procedures would work and how the whole process would be monitored.

In autumn 1992, the Government (in the 'Foster-Laming' letter) set out a range of 'key tasks' which local and health authorities were to carry out before April 1993. Community care plans for 1993 should have reflected these by showing:

- what resources health and local authorities expected to devote to community care in 1992–93 and 1993–94;

- services expected to be available, and changes planned for existing services;

- details of assessment arrangements;

- arrangements for purchase of residential and nursing home care;

- charging policies and arrangements for financial assessments;
- details of agreements between health and local authorities, particularly those for purchase of nursing home care, assessment arrangements and hospital discharge;
- details of agreements with housing authorities;
- how the plan had taken account of new GP fundholder purchasing responsibilities;
- how client choice would be taken into account;
- how the public would be informed about local implementation of the 1993 changes.[17]

In 1993 two further letters from the Department of Health Social Services Inspectorate and the NHS Management Executive (the 'Laming-Langlands' letters) summarised progress to date and highlighted areas where further work was needed. The March 1993 letter described further 'key tasks'. These included

- increasing the involvement of service users and carers;
- developing assessment and care management systems;
- further developing joint work between health and social services;
- developing a positive relationship with providers;
- shifting the balance of resources towards non-residential care, and providing more respite care and support for carers;
- involving housing authorities and agencies.

The December 1993 letter reminded authorities that plans should be used to 'manage the market'. Authorities should learn more about providers' needs and give information in their plans about what services they were planning to buy. Health authorities were reminded of the importance of planning for increased community health provision, in view of the move away from hospital-based services to services for people in their own homes. Health authorities should work closely with local authorities in developing plans.[18]

As we have seen, two statutory Directions added to local authorities' legal requirements in relation to planning.

Early plans were intended to 'map' existing provision and to assess local needs. Later emphasis from the Government has been on 'market management', in other words on encouraging authorities to develop a framework for the 'mixed economy of care'. Each of these approaches requires skills in certain planning tasks, which we now look at in a little more detail.

## Assessing the needs of the population

For planning purposes, 'needs assessment' means finding out about the care needs of local people. (It has another meaning in the context of assessment and care management (see Chapter 4), where it refers to the assessment of an individual person's needs.)

Local authorities have been assessing the needs of their populations for a long time. In 1970 the Chronically Sick and Disabled Persons Act required authorities to discover the needs of disabled people in their areas, and to provide certain services for them. However, many local authorities were hard pressed to develop an accurate picture of need. Many did not give priority to the task, and most found it virtually impossible to keep information up to date.

It should in theory be easier now for local authorities to find out about local needs, and to build up profiles of the different client groups. New systems of information management should help authorities keep track of needs. Records can show who uses services, and what users think about them. Just as important, information can be collected about people who need services but do not use them. Over time, the aim is for authorities to develop a much better picture of who needs what in their areas.

Sir Roy Griffiths commented on the importance of good information systems in local authorities, and noted that at the time of his report such systems needed considerable improvement. Much effort has since been devoted to developing ways of gathering and using information about community care needs. Good practice guidance was issued in 1993 to help local authorities in this process.[19]

The good practice guidance defines needs as 'the ability of an individual or collection of individuals to benefit from care'. It shows that assessing population needs is a dynamic process, which is informed by statistical information about different client groups, the outcome of local surveys and research, consultation with groups of users and carers, or information collected by other organisations. As we see later (pp 73–74), the picture of local needs should change and develop as a result of the assessment and care management processes.

In its second monitoring report on the community care reforms, the Audit Commission shows that local authorities have made some progress in building 'partial' estimates of needs for different client groups. To date, 'systematic inclusion of information from practitioners and through information systems is more limited' (*Taking Stock*, p 16).

## Special factors

In assessing the needs of their local populations, local authorities should be looking out for special factors which may affect needs for community care – for instance the needs of people in rural or inner city areas.

It is useful to reflect for a moment on the sometimes neglected subject of rural needs. In some counties, up to 50 per cent of people live in the country. Yet many of the services they need are likely to be in towns, including doctors, dentists, opticians and hospitals, as well as mainstream shopping and leisure facilities.

**A voluntary worker** (in 1992): 'The elderly people living here have lived an almost feudal existence. Many have lived all their lives in small villages where they have worked for the big house or farm in tied cottages with low wages. Then the post office closes, the village store and school go, the young people emigrate. Buses are "uneconomic" and the doctor has relocated. They need to make a journey for every single thing they want.'

Two years later this same voluntary worker commented that the community care changes had brought improvements in some rural areas. The consultation process had brought a willingness to acknowledge the characteristics of people in rural communities.

**A voluntary worker** (in 1994): 'They express their needs differently. What's acceptable to them is different. We see evidence that the care workers are increasingly willing to listen and act accordingly.'

Local authority plans need to show how the special needs of rural populations are met, taking into account housing, health and transport provision as well as social services.

The numbers of homeless or transient people are also important for planning, as are the needs of people from black and ethnic minority communities.

**A London borough**'s 1992 community care plan presented evidence that members of black and ethnic minority communities were disproportionately represented among the most disadvantaged groups suffering unemployment, homelessness, poor housing conditions and the effects of disability, sickness and higher than average mortality rates. 'It is significant that much of the current information about available services is failing to reach this group of people and therefore has prevented them from having their needs met.'

To combat the problem, the borough set out steps for development. These included: a language policy; a disability strategy; drawing up new consultation guidelines; grant aid to the black and ethnic minority voluntary sector; recruitment of specialist staff; monitoring service delivery to ethnic minority users; and talking with members of ethnic minority communities about services appropriate to their needs and how best to publicise them.[20]

In order to check on these various special needs, the authority has worked to make sure that its consultation process allows different groups of people to express their views, as well as using facts and figures already available. Its 1994 community care plan shows population figures for each part of the borough and describes progress and problems to date. After a period of development work, two community care resource centres have opened for older people in need from the Asian and African-Caribbean communities. These centres will provide luncheon club, day centre, domiciliary care, health promotion and information services. Improvements in access to care homes appropriate for the needs of older people from black and ethnic minority communities have been more difficult to achieve. The authority continues to work towards this goal.

Despite the improvements in practice in some authorities, monitoring of community care planning continues to show that local authorities have a long way to go to build a good picture of the needs of their black and ethnic minority populations. For instance, 'Knowledge of the needs of black and minority ethnic people was limited in all authorities' (*Monitoring and Development. First Impressions*, p 3).

# Consultation

A major theme of community care planning is that it should involve consultation with users, carers and local organisations (see p 55). Consultation is often talked about but is not easy to do well. It needs to reach different groups of people, large and small. It must ensure that people understand what they are being consulted about, and that they have enough information about what is going on to comment both on existing services and on those they would like to see developed. It has to be able to take on board many different points of view – of individuals and the organisations representing them, and of service providers and planners in all sectors.

---

**THE NATIONAL USERS AND CARERS GROUP**

At a national level, the Department of Health has set up the National Users and Carers Group. Members of this group meet to share views and experiences of community care and the reforms. The Department of Health's publication *Information on Community Care post April '93: The concerns of users and carers* summarises the group's observations. The report gives examples of good and bad practice. It emphasises the importance of good communication, and the need for people providing information for users and carers to put themselves 'in the shoes of the recipients'.

---

If it is not to be just a 'paper exercise', the consultation process must show that it has responded to what was said – explaining, where necessary, why certain views have not been acted on. It needs to be an ongoing exercise, not just a one-off performance.

Seeking the views of users is an important part of consultation. In addition, consultation should include potential users who may not be using services now, perhaps because:

- They don't want to.
- They don't know about services, or they can't get out to find out about them.
- There isn't enough of a particular service to go round.
- They can't afford the charges.
- They live in sheltered or supported homes, where it is assumed that they will receive support.

■   They have relatives, friends or neighbours who provide the necessary help – carers, who, as we have seen, may be service users themselves.

Efforts have to be made to contact those who might not easily learn about the process. This means that information about plans should be available, affordable and understandable to all possible users, including:

■   people who can't get out of their homes;

■   people who are blind and/or deaf;

■   people who don't speak or read English;

■   people who can't use public transport;

■   people who don't understand social services jargon.

Experience has shown that some authorities have made great efforts to consult local people, holding open days, providing transport to meetings, offering respite support to enable carers to take part, and consulting users of day centres and other services. In other authorities, consultation has been patchy and not well thought through: not enough notice has been given of meetings, and the people being consulted have not had adequate information about what was being proposed.

Response to consultation has often varied between client groups. In some areas older people are not used to being consulted, or to expressing their views.

**A planner:** 'We found it difficult to identify the "elderly consumer". We held two days for elderly people, but by and large those who came were the workers who cared for them, such as nurses. We did encourage them to bring clients and carers, but generally they didn't come.'

Many users need help to learn how to express their views, and to learn how to take part in planning, so that they can be fully involved and not always have to rely on others to put their point of view. Authorities have to learn how to set up consultation so that users feel able to take part.

Recent research describes the many different approaches to involving older and disabled people in community care planning. The research stresses the ongoing nature of consultation – it is not just a 'one-off' exercise – but at the same time warns that consultation places considerable demands on those being consulted. There is also a danger that over time community care planning will become more routine, with committees and working parties replacing early widespread publicity and local meetings.[21]

Consultation must also involve other authorities and service providers from all sectors. Many local authorities appear to have succeeded in consulting local interests effectively, but some have been criticised for not consulting adequately with other sectors. In many areas the private sector has not been much involved in consultation about plans. This has sometimes occurred because there is no clear local organisation to consult, but at times it has also reflected local authorities' reluctance to work with private sector providers.

In general, voluntary organisations have been more involved, but many feel that local authority timescales for consultation have been unrealistic, and that inadequate information has been provided.

As we have seen, the Government has issued Directions to strengthen the role of the independent sector in planning. These reflect the concerns discussed here, as well as the Government's desire to move local authorities more quickly towards 'managing the market' in promotion of the 'mixed economy of care'.

Those wishing to be involved in planning sometimes perceive a difference between 'consultation' – perhaps being shown a plan *after* it has been written and invited to comment – and 'involvement', whereby the planning *process* involves users, carers and providers from all sectors on an ongoing basis. Generally, the former is more common than the latter.

The complexities of consultation also show the difficulty of preparing one community care plan to meet a range of needs. One monitoring report has commented on the need to consider the different audiences that may use community care plans, noting that one plan may not be able to meet the needs of purchasers and providers alongside those of service users, who may require a different type or form of information.[22]

At its best, consultation means the local authority taking account of and acting on the views of local people and organisations representing a wide range of interests. At its worst, it is simply something to be 'gone through' in order to fulfil the requirements of the planning exercise.

## Trying to meet users' needs

One *dilemma* for local authorities is the problem of raising expectations. If planning involves encouraging everyone to say what they need, there are bound to be disappointments if all the needs cannot be met.

**A planner** (in 1992): 'Our members [the Council] said this plan was full of expectations – we shouldn't raise expectations which cannot be met. But disabled people said to us, "How dare you not discuss our unmet needs with us?" Our committee will have to learn to tolerate the concept of unmet need, and to debate this with the people in need.'

Acting on the views of users inevitably involves compromise. It is clearly impossible to plan for every single person's individual needs – and different groups of service users may want very different things. But the aim is to move towards services that reflect the needs of users, rather than services that are provided for the convenience of those who organise them, or to match what professionals say people ought to want. The planning process should be a crucial part of this.

However, as well as being the means for finding out about local needs and stating what kind of help may be available, plans should also show how local authorities choose their priorities and plan to meet needs within available resources. This aspect of planning has proved difficult for some authorities.

The Audit Commission (*Taking Stock*) emphasises the importance of plans including detailed eligibility criteria for services (see Chapter 4) and of authorities costing their priorities.

# The importance of housing and transport in planning

We have seen that community care is about more than health and social services.

**A county council** in the Midlands recognised the extent of the cooperation that was needed: 'Involving all Departments is important because good quality community care includes a range of services, such as transport, employment, housing, libraries, education as well as those provided by Social Services. People with special needs should have equal access to all these services.'[23]

For older people housing and transport are often particularly important.

# Housing and community care planning

*Caring for People* refers briefly to the importance of housing, stating:

> If dependent people are to be helped to continue living in the community, then their homes must be places where it is possible to provide the care they need. The Government believes that housing is a vital component of community care and is often the key to independent living. para 3.5.1

The White Paper goes on to say: 'Social services authorities will need to work closely with housing authorities, housing associations and other providers of housing of all types in developing plans for a full and flexible range of housing' (para 3.5.4).

Housing services may be provided by the local authority or by housing associations. Private providers increasingly offer different types of retirement housing for purchase.

---

## HOUSING ASSOCIATIONS

Housing associations are non-profit-distributing organisations run by voluntary committees. Some cater for general needs, while others are more specialist. For instance, some organisations have special projects of and for people from black and ethnic minority groups.

The type of care arranged by housing associations is very varied, ranging from shared housing, where people have their own rooms but some shared facilities, to staffed hostels, sheltered accommodation and care homes.

---

Local authorities and housing associations can provide a place for people to move *to* – for instance from an unmodernised home with stairs to a ground-floor flat with special adaptations, or from a long-stay hospital to a group home. Local authorities can also provide help to improve or adapt a person's existing home. In some areas there is a home improvement agency service, sometimes called Staying Put or Care and Repair, which gives advice and practical assistance to people who need to repair, improve or adapt their homes. These schemes are run by local authorities, housing associations and a variety of voluntary organisations.

Despite the importance of housing to community care, many of the early community care plans gave it scant coverage. In September 1992 the Departments of the Environment and of Health issued a joint circular on housing and community care (DOE 10/92; LAC(92)12). This circular stressed the importance of cooperation between housing and social services authorities in preparing plans and in assessment procedures. The 'Foster-Laming' and subsequent letters (see pp 56–57) emphasised the need for housing to have a much higher profile in community care plans, and plans increasingly include reference to housing issues. Additional Government guidance aims to help local authorities make further progress.[24]

 ## Transport and community care planning

The crucial role played by transport in community care is acknowledged in the Practitioners' Guide, part of the Department of Health's Practice Guidance on assessment (see p 80):

> [Transport] is fundamental in enabling services to get to people or people to services. Failure to recognise its contribution can lead to false perceptions of need, for example, providing meals on wheels to someone who fails to cook because they have no means of reaching the shops.    Practitioners' Guide, p 59

Effective transport helps people to reach services – such as day care, day hospitals and outpatients departments. It is also important that carers and relatives should be able to visit people being cared for away from their own homes. For many people transport also provides the link with 'ordinary' life – shops, libraries, cinemas and other recreational facilities.

**A planner from a local authority:** 'The housing department's plan is included in the community care plan; but transport is still a gap – there isn't a policy on that.'

Research on assessment and care management re-emphasises the importance of transport for many people who need community care. For instance: 'Transport, its costs and the ways in which it helped or hindered people in their use of other services featured very strongly in our interviews. A choice of services is of very little use if one cannot get to them or if getting to them becomes an ordeal.'[25] The Audit Commission also shows that transport is a major theme raised repeatedly by users and carers in discussing their community care needs (*Taking Stock*).

# Negotiating planning agreements

Another task for the local authority is to negotiate planning agreements with local health authorities. These agreements are statements that they have agreed common goals for services, have made funding agreements, and have decided who will do what.

Such planning agreements are now an essential part of community care in any local area. They should ensure that disputes do not arise between health and local authorities. If, for example, a local authority wants to increase the numbers of older people who can be cared for in their own homes, it may make arrangements for sitting services to relieve carers, for day care, and for social work support for older people and their families. At the same time, the authority will rely on the relevant health authority or fundholding GP to arrange appropriate nursing services, incontinence provision and physiotherapy. There needs to be agreement about how this will work, but early evidence shows that community health services have been slow to respond in many areas.

In Chapter 2 we described some of the complexities of local and health authority structures. Many social services and health authorities are not 'coterminous'. In other words, they do not have the same boundaries. There may be several health authorities within one local authority, or a health authority may cover part of several metropolitan boroughs. In addition to having different boundaries, the various authorities have their own customs, cultures and organisational structures, so one local authority may be dealing with several very different health authorities and with many fundholding GPs.

## JOINT WORKING: HEALTH AND SOCIAL SERVICES

Planning agreements may be made easier by the existence in some areas of joint working, through Joint Consultative Committees or Joint Care Planning Teams. Such bodies bring together health and social services officers and workers to promote cooperative working – either in the authorities as a whole or, for instance, with reference to a particular client group, such as older people, people with learning disabilities or people with mental health problems. Joint strategy groups may be working on joint commissioning by health and social services, and guidance to help such collaboration is being developed by the Department of Health.

**Joint finance** is often used for projects run by the NHS, social services or voluntary organisations, but involving cooperation and budget-sharing between them. In a few areas it has been used to fund joint training, with the aim of developing effective joint working of staff from different agencies. This is a way of crossing the sometimes artificial barriers between health and social services.

The negotiation of planning agreements is a complex task. From 1993 such agreements should have covered the assessment of care needs, the provision of continuing care, including respite care, in residential and nursing homes, and training strategies – Government guidance encourages the development of joint training between statutory authorities and independent sector organisations.

The Managers' Guide (see p 80) on care management and assessment discusses what may be involved. It notes that the 1990 Act places a formal duty on local authorities to bring apparent health care needs to the attention of the appropriate health authority, and states that 'health profes-

## COMMUNITY CARE CHARTERS

In addition to cooperation in planning, local authorities must work with health, housing and other local organisations to prepare community care charters. A *Framework for Local Community Care Charters in England* was published by the Department of Health in November 1994. It states that local authorities, together with health and housing authorities, will have to produce local community care charters by April 1996.

The Government states that these charters will be a 'first step to ensuring that charter principles and standards are reflected in the way that authorities actually perform their functions'. Community care plans should 'draw on and be consistent with local charters' (para 16).

There should be wide and open consultation on community care charters, perhaps linked to that for community care plans. Charters should include:

*a statement of authorities' commitment to high quality, well coordinated services;*

*specific standards, as tightly defined as possible, to which services will be delivered and monitored.*                                          (para 13)

The charter *Framework* sets out a range of 'expectations' for local service users, but despite urging from many national voluntary organisations during consultation on the *Framework*, the Government has not introduced *national* standards for community care. Despite the impact of national policies on community care, the Government stresses its local nature and the importance of having local charters.

Charters should be published jointly by all the authorities involved. It remains to be seen how they will influence cooperation between authorities and providers at local level, and how they will influence people's experience of community care.

sionals are expected to identify social care needs and advise patients appropriately. Community care plans should spell out how the two agencies will put this duty into effect' (para 4.17).

The Managers' Guide goes on to discuss the negotiation which should be involved in devising collaborative care management and assessment procedures – which will affect community care planning:

> In England, local authorities will have to engage with both District Health Authorities and Family Health Services Authorities as the purchasing authorities. There may also be direct negotiation between local authorities and provider units, such as NHS Trusts, where these offer social care facilities. The way that fundholding general practitioners deploy their budgets may also have an impact on the profile of community care services at the local level so they, too, should be party to such negotiations.          para 4.18

## Defining responsibilities for 'health' and 'social' care

Negotiating planning agreements requires health and local authorities to face the difficult task of defining their respective responsibilities for 'health' and 'social' care.

In practice, distinguishing between health and social care is not always easy. Home helps or home carers often carry out 'nursing' tasks, such as administering drugs or changing dressings and colostomy bags. Occupational therapists – often in short supply – may work for health or local authorities. Bathing services are often disputed territory between health and social services, as noted in a report from Age Concern Greater London:

> Few would argue with the premise that to keep oneself clean is a fundamental need and not a luxury . . . Elderly people who cannot bath themselves appear to be falling through a gap between their health authority district nursing service and their local authority social services, with neither authority willing to admit responsibility for running the service.[26]

The National Association of Health Authorities and Trusts (NAHAT) has published a report describing a project which attempted to define 'health' and 'social' tasks. It emphasised the importance of avoiding disputes about who should do what, while stressing the need to identify who should be responsible, and who should pay for different services. It recognised that such definitions are useful as a guide, 'but will not resolve all of those very difficult situations where there is inter-authority disagreement about responsibilities for a number of particular individual cases'.[27]

**A social services officer:** 'To me I don't think it's where medical services end or social services begin. Because I don't think you can package people. But there are grey areas in between, and I think we have to work together to find out where they are. A lot of people are on the edges of health and social care. Their needs can change from one to the other and we have to allow ourselves not to be constricted by artificial divisions.'

To break down some of the barriers between 'health' and 'social' care, Griffiths referred in his report to the creation of a new type of worker – a 'community carer'. He suggested that community carers might take on the work of some home helps or home care assistants, community nursing assistants and residential care staff (Griffiths Report, para 8.4).

However such work is done, the Managers' Guide for care management and assessment makes clear that negotiations at local level will be crucial:

> The Government has not thought it appropriate to attempt to define a rigid demarcation between health and social care; the interface between the two is for local discussion and agreement.  para 4.20

It is to avoid potential disputes that the Government has urged health and local authorities to make clear planning agreements showing who will do what. Indeed, for nursing home provision, the Government has *required* local authorities to show how they have reached agreement with health authorities about their respective responsibilities as a condition of receiving funds transferred from the social security budget in 1993 and 1994. A condition of receiving those funds in 1995 is that health and local authorities should review – and where appropriate amend – existing agreements on their respective responsibilities for continuing care, and on how hospital discharge agreements will be integrated with assessment arrangements.

In Chapter 8 we discuss responsibility for continuing care, which relates to the division between 'health' and 'social' care. Nearly all monitoring of the first year or more of the reformed system shows that the 'health–social care divide' remains problematic. For example, the Association of Directors of Social Services has commented on the problems that arise,[28] and local authorities themselves seek a clearer definition of responsibilities from central government (see, for example, *Implementing*

*Caring for People. Community care packages for elderly people*, published by the Department of Health).

## Setting targets

Early plans focused on the definition of aims and objectives for services and setting *measurable* targets for services to aim for, and time limits for meeting them. These can be genuine expressions of new goals, although in practice they may often amount to not much more than vague statements of good intentions. Targets might include:

- ensuring that everyone assessed as being of a particular dependency level has access to a certain amount of services;
- achieving a certain staffing level for services;
- providing a certain number of day care places;
- improving cooperation between services;
- preparing a report on one aspect of services, such as enhancing equality of opportunity.

The limitation of targets is that they tend to relate to easily measurable aspects of a service – for instance, the number of home carers per 1,000 people aged 75 or over. Even if you know this target has been met, this will not necessarily tell you how *good* the service is. Targets are set in the Patient's Charter, for instance, for waiting times in outpatient departments. Clearly no one wants to be kept waiting longer than necessary, and it is important that patients know what has caused a wait. However, a short wait does not necessarily mean that the appointment has gone well. Thus targets may not tell us much about the *quality* of services, unless they include a way of measuring quality as well as quantity – such as interviewing a certain number of service users to find out how they feel about the service in question. (The Audit Commission also sets targets for local authorities under the Citizen's Charter initiative. The problem arises with some of these targets too.)

## Choosing priorities

Setting targets means choosing priorities. We have seen that one of the Government's main aims is to ensure that services are as effective and as efficient as possible in meeting needs, given the resources that are available. This means that some needs will be identified which cannot be met.

Part of the purpose of the consultation process, and of negotiating with everyone involved, is to decide which needs should have greatest priority.

A major aim of the White Paper is that services should be targeted on those in greatest need. How such need is identified locally will depend on the eligibility criteria which the authority sets and the priorities chosen, but must take into account the statutory duties which local authorities already have to provide certain services (see p 52). There is no hard and fast rule about how priorities are set. This is one reason why a good consultation process is so important. Without one, the priorities chosen may simply reflect the needs of those who shout the loudest, perhaps neglecting the needs of vulnerable but less vocal people.

## The targeting dilemma

There is a dilemma here. Targeting services seems to make good sense. It should direct resources where the needs are greatest. For older people, this is often said to mean those who are at risk of having to leave their own homes because of growing care needs. Targeting resources on such people may help them remain at home for as long as possible, but may be at the expense of people with lower levels of need who were formerly receiving some help.

Many authorities are already well down the road to increased 'targeting'. Their plans illustrate moves towards providing more intensive services to fewer people. Some former users of services have been very much taken by surprise when their service has been withdrawn. One woman wrote to the social services department about her mother, aged 93, whose home help was withdrawn, despite health problems:

> I note that services have been cut by 25 per cent. Twenty-five per cent of four hours per week, the service my mother was receiving, is one hour, leaving three hours per week. Perhaps you can explain why my mother's service has been cut by 100 per cent! . . . I feel you are particularly short-sighted. In my mother's case, you could, with a little more thought and organisation, have cut her service by 50 per cent not 100 per cent. As it is, if this coming winter is anything like the last, my mother may have to apply for residential care, at a time when I was under the impression you would rather keep people in their own homes with help.

**A home care organiser:** 'There are changed criteria now because of the budget. There's no preventive work done, and if you don't do the preventive work, the person becomes a crisis. If you take the service away and if the family don't come in (and a lot of elderly people don't have a family) you've got a crisis.'

Some people are concerned that focusing mainly on the people with the greatest needs is leading to neglect of those who have *some* care needs, but who are not yet *very* dependent. It could be that those who can afford to will be able to buy in services for themselves, leaving less well-off people unable to buy services or obtain them from the local authority. It is important to remember that some such people may have rights under the Chronically Sick and Disabled Persons Act (see p 79).

Targeting also affects carers. In some areas people living alone are given highest priority, along with those whose carers are very stressed. This could mean that some carers do not receive the support they need to carry on.

# MONITORING AND REVIEW

All aspects of the community care reforms should feed back into a monitoring and review system. Like planning, monitoring and review should really be part of most kinds of work. Also like planning, it is easy to neglect this. Frequently, service providers who think they do a good job do not see the point of monitoring and reviewing what they do. They can get stuck in a particular pattern if they do not constantly check on how they are doing and think about ways of improving their work.

Local authorities are required to monitor and review their community care plans each year. This should mean that they look at all parts of their community care work on a continuous basis. They should be drawing on the information they obtain from, for instance, the consultation, assessment and care management, inspection and complaints processes, and constantly checking on how their contracts are working out. After community care charters come into place in 1996 authorities will have to publish information about their performance.

At a national level, the first community care plans were monitored by the Department of Health Social Services Inspectorate (SSI). It published regional reports about how all the community care reforms were working, and offered advice and guidance to local authorities whose plans did not look like meeting the key objectives of the White Paper over a reasonable time. The SSI can advise the Secretary of State for Health, who has the power under the NHS and Community Care Act to intervene to make sure that 'local authorities' plans are in line with national policies and priorities, and that implementation is proceeding at a reasonable pace' (Policy Guidance, para 2.21).

In 1994–95 local authorities used a questionnaire developed by the Social Services Inspectorate to monitor their own progress in implementation.[29] They should have involved local provider organisations and service users and carers in this process. The aim was to encourage authorities to focus on aspects of their work which need improvement and development, in consultation with their local populations. In some areas, however, it is not clear just how effective this local consultation was.

In theory, the monitoring and review process should offer everyone concerned – service users, carers, voluntary and private providers, local tax-payers – a chance to have their say about how they think things are working. The consultation process, the assessment procedure, and the complaints and inspection processes provide other opportunities. A record should be kept of how people feel about what is provided – or about what they feel they need. This record should be made publicly available. To date evidence shows that this 'monitoring information loop' is not well developed. If it were, it would give users and others in the community better information through which to exercise their powers as citizens.

For instance, they might want to try to persuade the relevant authorities to put resources into new initiatives, or they might find that there simply were not enough resources available. They might then want to contact their local Member of Parliament and the Government of the day, to lobby for more resources to be made available from central funds. Every four years they can vote on who runs their local authority services.

---

Local authorities' community care plans have changed each year. From early attempts to state what they *hoped* to achieve for various client groups, they have evolved in a variety of ways. In many authorities, it is necessary to read the plans together, as they do not repeat the information given in previous years.

Part of the reason for the change in the content and style of plans has been the Government's revised instructions to local authorities. We have seen that these include a new emphasis on managing the market – on plans as a purchasing tool – and on ensuring that independent sector providers know about local authorities' plans for buying services so that they can prepare to offer appropriate provision.

One problem for many authorities has been the timescale within which plans must be prepared and published. Local authorities' financial and planning years begin in April. Final budgets are generally agreed in January, when the amount of central government grant is known (see Chapter 8). This means that authorities are developing and consulting on their plans during the previous autumn. They are encouraged to set specific spending and service provision targets before they know how much money they will have each year. There have been some suggestions that the timescale for planning should be revised to take these factors into account.

Community care plans fulfil a number of purposes. As well as serving to help 'manage the market', they are important in enabling local people to take a continuing part in the planning process. To do so, they must know that such plans exist, and where to find them. They need to be able to find out what has happened to proposals in the previous plan, and how consultation is carried out for the next one. In this way, the community care plans should be the beginning and end of the yearly cycle of planning for and providing services.

The timing of plans, the importance of consultation and cooperation in preparing plans, and updated details of what they should contain are included in draft guidance on planning issued in early 1995 (*Community care plans for 1996–97 in England*). The draft guidance also places importance on longer-term strategic planning, using 'rolling medium to long term plans' in cooperation with health and housing authorities.

# 4 Assessment and Care Management

One aim of the community care reforms is to make sure that publicly supported services are provided on the basis of a proper assessment of needs. Assessment is the first step in the process of care management – of sorting out needs, deciding whether services can be arranged, devising a 'package of care' as part of a 'care plan', and reviewing the situation from time to time.

Following the reforms, local authorities have faced increasing demand for services, leading to increased pressure to carry out their new duty to assess people needing community care services. Many questions have arisen about exactly what an assessment is – or should be – and whether assessments showing needs for certain services should bring automatic entitlement to them.

The respective roles of health and social services in assessment have been the focus of much monitoring of the reforms. Links with general practitioners have been examined. Monitoring has also noted the pressures to carry out assessments at the time of hospital discharge, which has sometimes meant that it is quicker and easier for people in hospital to get an assessment than it is for people who might have similar needs living elsewhere.

In this chapter we look at what the White Paper, the Act and the guidance say about assessments and the process of care management. In doing so we discuss some of the many issues which increasingly surround assessment as the focus of the reformed system, including the relationship between assessment, eligibility criteria, decisions about needs, and resources.

# LOCAL AUTHORITIES' LEGAL DUTIES

## The White Paper and the Act

*Caring for People* spelt out the duty of local authorities to assess people needing 'social care and support – eg for mobility, personal care, domestic tasks, financial affairs, accommodation, leisure and employment, which they cannot arrange for themselves' (para 3.2.2).

> Assessment should take account of the wishes of the individual and his or her carer, and of the carer's ability to continue to provide care ... efforts should be made to offer flexible services which enable individuals and carers to make choices. *Caring for People*, para 3.2.6

The NHS and Community Care Act made assessment of need for 'community care services' a duty for local authorities. Where it appears to an authority that 'any person for whom they may provide or arrange for the provision of community care services may be in need of any such services' the authority must carry out an assessment of needs for services and decide whether these needs call for provision of such services (section 47(1)(a) and (b)).

For the purposes of the Act, community care services are those which local authorities can provide under the following Acts: Part III of the National Assistance Act; section 45 of the Health Services and Public Health Act 1968; section 21 of and Schedule 8 to the National Health Service Act 1977; and section 117 of the Mental Health Act 1983. (These are described in Appendix 2.)

The duty to assess is linked with the transfer of social security funds to local authorities, and is meant to ensure that publicly supported care in care homes is provided on the basis of an assessment of need. Assessment should also identify people who can best be helped to remain in their own homes, with appropriate support.

## Who is eligible for assessment?

People who 'appear to need community care services' are eligible. Local authorities must publish information about eligibility for assessment and for services (Policy Guidance, para 3.18). This information should be prepared in cooperation with health and housing authorities, and with other service providers. It should include:

- how and where to apply for an assessment;
- who is eligible for assessment;
- how the authority will decide who is eligible for services;
- how to make representations and complaints;
- details about the care services available in residential and nursing homes and in people's own homes, provided by all sectors.

The information should be available to anyone who needs it, and should take account of the needs of people who do not speak English, who have various cultural backgrounds, or who have difficulty communicating.

Each local authority has its own system for assessment and provision of services. This means that people living in different parts of the country are covered by different procedures – with the exception of the charging procedures for residential and nursing home care (see pp 157–163).

# The existing rights of disabled people

If, during an assessment under the 1990 Act, an authority finds that a person should be considered as a 'disabled person', the NHS and Community Care Act states that the authority must also assess the person under the provisions of the Disabled Persons (Services, Consultation and Representation) Act 1986, and tell the person about their rights under that Act. In order to understand the provisions of the Act, it is necessary to look briefly at some earlier legislation. The National Assistance Act defines the people who are eligible for services under the Chronically Sick and Disabled Persons Act.

## The National Assistance Act 1948

Section 29 of the National Assistance Act 1948, as amended, gave local authorities a general duty to promote the welfare of certain people. They were defined (in England) as:

> Persons aged 18 or over who are blind, deaf or dumb or who suffer from mental disorder of any description and other persons aged 18 or over who are substantially and permanently handicapped by illness, injury or congenital deformity or such other disabilities as are described by the Minister.

Circular LAC(93)10 shows that partially sighted and hard of hearing people are also included in this definition. This circular brings together many older pieces of guidance, and includes Approvals and Directions to local authorities about carrying out their powers and duties under sections 21 and 29 of the 1948 Act.

## The Chronically Sick and Disabled Persons Act 1970

The Chronically Sick and Disabled Persons (CSDP) Act 1970 describes more specifically the services to be provided under the general duty set out in section 29 of the National Assistance Act. Section 2 lists services to be provided where the local authority is 'satisfied' that they are needed and that they will meet the needs of the disabled person. In summary, they are:

- practical assistance in the home;

- provision of, or assistance in obtaining, radio, television, library or similar recreational facilities;

- recreational facilities outside the home, or help in taking advantage of educational facilities;

- facilities for, or assistance in, travelling to and from home to participate in any services provided by the local authority under section 29 of the National Assistance Act, or similar services (eg sheltered employment);

- assistance in arranging for any works of adaptation in the home or the provision of additional facilities designed to secure greater safety, comfort or convenience;

- facilities for taking holidays;

- meals at home or elsewhere;

- provision of, or assistance in obtaining, a telephone and any special equipment necessary to enable use of a telephone.

The Act also requires local authorities to find out how many disabled people live in their area and to keep a register of such people. (Circular LAC(93)10 (Appendix 2, para 2.3) directs local authorities to keep such registers.) This is what we mean when we talk about someone being 'registered as disabled', but people do not have to be 'registered' in order to receive services under the Act.

### The Disabled Persons Act 1986

Section 4 of the Disabled Persons (Services, Representation and Consultation) Act 1986 then gave local authorities a duty to assess people for services which could be provided under the CSDP Act, if asked to do so by the disabled person, his or her representative, or a carer. Section 8 requires the local authority, when making an assessment, to consider the ability of a carer to continue to provide care on a regular basis. (See Appendix 1.)

The community care assessment process must take account of people's rights under these Acts.

# The 1990 legislation

Local authorities thus already had a duty to assess the individual needs of disabled people when requested, and to provide certain services for them. The 1990 Act (section 47(2)) adds to this by saying that a disabled person must be assessed under that Act *without* the authority being requested to do so, and that people who appear to need community care services must also be assessed.

None of the Acts shows how 'needs' should be defined, nor are there stated levels of service which should be provided under the authority's various legal duties. This means that the variation in provision which has always existed between authorities will continue, and that it is difficult to say how much of a particular service should be available for a particular person.

Despite the fact that we do not have hard and fast ways of judging if, or how much of, a service should be available, we can look at what the Government has said about local authorities setting up assessment and care management processes. We have already mentioned the Policy Guidance, which says what is expected of local authorities. The Practice Guidance gives much more detail about how local authorities might develop this work. The Practice Guidance on care management and assessment appeared in three volumes, a Summary, a Practitioners' Guide, and a Managers' Guide. (The Summary is also included in the latter two volumes.) The rest of this chapter looks at aspects of assessment and care management, referring frequently to the Practice Guidance and to evidence about how the system is developing.

# THE ASSESSMENT AND CARE MANAGEMENT PROCESS

Once the local authority has decided to assess someone, the guidance suggests that it should go through several steps. These form the process of care management and are described in the Practitioners' Guide:

**deciding the level of assessment**

**assessing needs**

**deciding whether to arrange services to help meet these needs**

**developing a care plan**

**carrying out the care plan**

**checking on – or monitoring – how things are going**

**reviewing the assessment and the plan**

## Deciding the level of assessment (screening)

The Practitioners' Guide says that 'the assessment process should be as simple, speedy and informal as possible . . . based on the principle of what is the least that it is necessary to know to understand the needs being presented and to justify the investment of public resources' (para 3.3).

The Practitioners' Guide describes six levels of assessment which authorities might use, from 'simple' assessments for people requiring, say, a bus pass, which is available from a single agency under clearly defined rules; to a 'limited' assessment, again for a single need, but requiring consideration of certain criteria, say for low-level support at home; to a 'comprehensive' assessment, for severe, multiple needs and a high level of risk, requiring the cooperation of several agencies and services from different sources. In practice most authorities have settled for three levels, broadly described as simple, specialist and comprehensive. Deciding which level is appropriate is often referred to as 'screening'.

Some uncertainty has arisen about the extent to which 'screening' actually constitutes an assessment. Sometimes when people telephone social services about a problem, they may receive the response that the needs described do not come within the authority's eligibility criteria for services. In this way the screening process can jump from the request for help to a decision about 'eligibility for services'. Some people can thus miss out on an assessment (which in theory should be available to anyone who may need a community care service).

The Practitioners' Guide tries to avoid this happening by suggesting that checklists, or 'trigger' questions, may be useful in discovering if there is a deeper need than that which the person presents. Many local authorities have introduced special training for reception staff or other workers who

## FACTORS TO BE TAKEN INTO ACCOUNT IN A COMPREHENSIVE

The Practitioners' Guide (pp 58–59) suggests the following as a comprehensive assessment guideline. This shows the range of information which could be gathered over time in complex situations. Obtaining such information is a skilled and time-consuming task.

**Biographical details**
Age, family circumstances, religion and ethnic origin.

**Self-perceived needs**

**Self care**
How well the person can carry out basic tasks such as eating, dressing or bathing; how well they can get around.

**Physical health**
Checking whether a request for social care arises from a health need which could be improved.

**Mental health**
Checking to see whether a mental health need has developed unnoticed or unreported. The assessor will have to judge when it is appropriate to consult a health worker, such as the GP or a community psychiatric nurse.

**Use of medicines**
Checking to see if there are problems in taking essential medicines, and whether a pharmacist, GP or nurse should be involved.

**Abilities, attitudes and lifestyle**
Checking the person's situation in relation to their own expectations.

**Race and culture**
Appreciating racial and cultural diversity when identifying individual needs and how to deal with them.

**Personal history**
Making sure that the effects of past events – perhaps a bereavement – are fully taken into account in assessing present needs.

**Needs of carers**
Carers should always be aware of their entitlement to be involved and to be consulted (within the constraints of confidentiality). It should never be assumed that carers will have the same views about needs and care as

are responsible for finding out about the needs of people who approach social services, and for making sure that such people are put in touch with other relevant services and receive appropriate assessment.

**Mr O'Malley** lives close to local shops and a library. He has difficulty coping with the stairs and with some aspects of his personal care. He contacts the social services department, which decides that he needs an assessment – but not urgently.

## ASSESSMENT

the person being assessed – the assessor will have to weigh up the different views.

### Social network and support
What other help is available, apart from immediate carers?

### Care services
What services are already being received, and how appropriate are they now?

### Housing
Housing authorities and/or other providers (such as housing associations) should always be involved in the assessment if there may be a housing need.

### Transport
Some needs may arise because of lack of suitable transport – for instance to get to the shops.

### Risk
Different kinds of risk may be involved – for instance those caused by certain health conditions, such as diabetes or epilepsy; those caused by environmental hazards, such as the use of gas by people with dementing illnesses; or behavioural risks, such as threatening behaviour. The person being assessed may wish to accept certain risks which their families, perhaps, feel are unacceptable. Neighbours may be concerned about dangers with the use of gas. The assessor will have to weigh up these risks, with emphasis given to the person's entitlement to self-determination and independence (always bearing in mind that person's capacity to take informed decisions).

### Finance
Assessors will be urged to make sure that the person being assessed and their carer(s) receive all the benefits to which they are entitled. Assessors will also have to test the means of the person being assessed, to see how much, if anything, they should pay towards the cost of care.

This would probably initially fit into a limited – or simple – assessment category. It seems that it would involve only one person from the social services department, although if further problems are revealed it could need a more detailed approach.

**Mr and Mrs Singh** live in a first-floor council flat with no lift. Mrs Singh suffers from senile dementia; Mr Singh has a heart condition. Carrying groceries, coping with housework and caring for his wife are becoming increasingly difficult. Their son lives ten miles away with his wife and three young children. They are able to offer support at weekends.

Mr and Mrs Singh have more complex problems. They need support for Mrs Singh and they really need rehousing. Mr Singh would like someone to sit with his wife once a week, while he attends the social evening at the local club. The assessment needs to take into account both their own circumstances and the contribution their family are willing and able to make to their care. They may need advice about benefits they could claim. Special attention should be paid to the needs of Mr Singh, as his wife's carer. He wants to go on caring for her, but if his health eventually breaks down this will not be possible.

This might be a specialist assessment – not quite as complicated as a 'complex' or 'comprehensive' assessment, which is described in the Practitioners' Guide as being for high-risk situations, with severe or very complex needs.

Comprehensive – and other higher-level – assessments may involve many people in what is called multidisciplinary cooperation. Such work is often talked about, but it is not always easy to put into practice. Different professionals and other workers have varied backgrounds and training, and need to learn to build trust in the judgement of people from different disciplines in order to make their own distinct contribution, yet avoid overlapping or unnecessary duplication of work.

The Managers' Guide discusses the important role which can be played in assessment by GPs and their staff, community nurses, and therapy services. Government guidance on training (*Training for the Future*) shows how important a joint approach to training can be in helping workers and managers to learn to work together and to develop common values and skills.

The Social Services Inspectorate's monitoring teams and others have commented on the need for good multidisciplinary cooperation in assessment, and the difficulty in achieving it:

> Although it was said there were good models of hospital social workers involving hospital medical and nursing staff in assessments, this multidisciplinary input was generally not reported at community level and required further development.
>
> *Implementing Caring for People. Community care packages for older people*, para 5.9

In recent years there has been increasing awareness of the need for people carrying out assessments to consider whether there has been abuse of older people, and wherever vulnerable older people are being cared for. Such abuse could be physical or emotional, or it could be financial abuse where someone is mishandling an older person's funds. A new charity, Action on Elder Abuse (address on p 198), is bringing together a wide range of workers and organisations to consider the many issues involved, and to develop better practice in identifying abuse of older people. See also ACE Books' publication *Old Age Abuse* (details on p 210).

# Assessing needs

One problem with assessments has been confusion between deciding the 'level' of assessment and the consequent findings about needs. Sometimes the needs are judged before the assessment is offered, and the level of assessment is then decided according to what the needs are expected to be. This confusion in the process may interfere with the statement in the Summary of the Practice Guidance that:

> Care management makes the needs and wishes of users and carers central to the caring process. This needs-led approach aims to tailor services to individual requirements.
>
> para 19

The assessments of Mr O'Malley and of Mr and Mrs Singh should ideally be carried out with their needs as they see them firmly in mind. It has been argued that in the past people have often been fitted to the services, rather than services made to meet the needs of the people using them.

However, the views of users and carers may differ: a carer may want regular breaks – periods of respite – whereas the person being cared for might not want to be looked after by anyone else. The Summary of the Practice Guidance states that if there is a significant problem, it may be appropriate to assess the carer's needs separately (para 39). Indeed, at the time of writing, carers' organisations are campaigning, through a Private Members Bill in Parliament, for carers to have a right to an assessment for themselves. (See p 193 for rights which carers already have under the Disabled Persons Act 1986.)

The Practitioners' Guide recommends that as far as possible users should participate actively in their own assessment. In practice, some users and carers are often not even aware that they have been 'assessed'. In addition, some people are not able to express their views, or take an active part. Their ability to communicate might be impaired through accident or mental disorder or they may not be able to speak English. Such people may need an *advocate* or *interpreter*, or access to a sign language or lip-reading service. Local authorities should give people information

| ADVOCACY |
| --- |

An advocate speaks *on behalf of* someone, as if they were speaking *for* that person. If the advocate knew the person before they became ill or disabled, they may well know what views the person would have. If not, the advocate will have to befriend the person, and try to find out by various means what the person would want for themselves.

Advocacy is important in representing the interests of people who are unable to make decisions for themselves, or who need support to have their say. *Self-advocacy* brings together groups of people to help them state their own views. *Citizen advocacy* provides trained ordinary citizens as advocates to represent the interests of people who need help in expressing their own views. People with learning disabilities and with mental health problems have historically had decisions made for them.

An advocate is not the same as an interpreter. An *interpreter* simply repeats what the person is saying.

The availability of advocates and interpreters is an important part of equal opportunities – ensuring that people are not disadvantaged by not being able to communicate with the people providing services or carrying out assessments.

If implemented, section 1 of the Disabled Persons Act 1986 would give local authorities the power to appoint an advocate for someone who cannot appoint his or her own representative because of any physical or mental incapacity. Section 2 would require the local authority to permit an authorised representative to act for a disabled person, at their request. However, these sections of the Act are not in force, even though they have been passed in law (see Appendix 1 for further description of the Act).

about local advocacy schemes if this seems appropriate; the guidance recommends that interpreters should be available if needed.

The Managers' Guide discusses different ways in which local authorities might make advocacy available to people who need it, suggesting that local authorities will wish to target their resources on users with a priority need, for example:

> users unable to express their own views who have no acceptable friend or relative to act on their behalf;
>
> users who are in dispute with the agency;
>
> users who have been previously disadvantaged, for example, minority ethnic users or disabled people.                                                      para 2.49

Especially for those users who are unable to request such assistance, there should be agreed criteria for triggering the involvement of advocacy support (para 2.50).

## Cooperation with health and housing authorities

The Act says that local authorities must inform the relevant authorities if people who ask them for assessment have health or housing needs.

Such communication is essential, for instance, in the case of Mr and Mrs Singh. It is likely that they will need to find more suitable accommodation, perhaps in sheltered housing. They also have health needs which are likely to increase. The assessment process needs to take these into account at an early stage, so that any proposals for their care will have the full cooperation of all those involved. Any 'package of care' which is devised for them must be agreed by all the agencies involved.

The local authority cannot assess someone as needing a nursing home place without agreement of the health authority. This is an important area for clear definitions of responsibility, as we discuss on pages 172–174.

As we have already noted, the links between health and social services have been a major theme of almost all monitoring exercises related to the community care reforms. The different cultures of 'health' and 'social' services are particularly discussed in one Social Services Inspectorate report, *Implementing Caring for People. The role of the GP and primary healthcare team*, which fully discusses the many issues involved. This report shows the importance of joint training, which should ideally be based in GP practices. It also discusses the importance of better communication between social services and primary health care teams; the need to develop joint strategies to reach ethnic minority communities; and the importance of better links when carrying out assessments and making decisions about care, in particular at the time of hospital discharge or admission to NHS continuing care or other types of care.

## Confidentiality

Communication with other authorities and organisations should give due regard to the need for confidentiality. This applies equally to the health service and other authorities. People need to know that their affairs will not be discussed without their permission. The Policy Guidance states that most communication between workers, such as between social workers and GPs, should take place informally – perhaps by telephone. Only in relatively complex cases should there be formal case conferences (para 3.35).

This makes it all the more important that people's privacy is protected, and that users of services know how local authorities and others will use and respect information about them. Some processes are regulated by law. The Data Protection Act 1984, for example, is designed to make sure that computerised information relating to an individual is obtained fairly, kept up to date and stored securely. The person has a right of access to check the accuracy of the information. Confidentiality is protected by other Acts and circulars which are listed in the Policy Guidance. These include the Access to Personal Files Act 1987 and the Access to Health Records Act 1990. At the time of writing, the Government is considering new guidance on confidentiality of personal health information.

The Practitioners' Guide gives the following 'Principles of Confidentiality':

Information should be used only for the purposes for which it was given.

Information about a user/patient should normally be shared only with the consent of that person.

Information should be shared on a 'need to know' basis.

Users and carers should be advised why and with whom information concerning them has been shared.

All confidential information should be rigorously safeguarded.             para 1.21

The Government's *Framework for Local Community Care Charters in England* states that users and their carers are entitled to expect confidentiality and that personal information will be protected.

## Where are assessments carried out?

Assessments are carried out wherever is most appropriate. This could be in a person's home, including a care home, or in hospital after a fall or serious illness. In some cases assessments may happen over a period of days or weeks. (Indeed, some observers have expressed the view that assessment for people with changing needs, or in the early stages of new dependency, should really be thought of as a more drawn-out, continuous process, or updated at specific intervals.[30])

Part of the assessment could take place in hospital, for instance, with further assessment carried out later. It should, however, be remembered that guidance on hospital discharge states that appropriate services should be in place, or firm plans made, before discharge. The Department of Health has published a *Hospital Discharge Workbook*, setting out good practice in carrying out hospital discharge.

As we have seen, health and local authorities are required to show that they have agreed about how people will be assessed when they leave hospital, either to return to their current home or to move to somewhere more appropriate for their needs. This also involves health and local authorities agreeing their respective responsibilities to provide services.

## Who carries out the assessment?

At present, assessment and care management tasks are carried out by different types of people in different authorities. According to the Social Services Inspectorate's 1993 monitoring report, *First Impressions, April–September 1993*, 'Authorities were sorting out which posts – social worker, district nurse, occupational therapist, community psychiatric nurse – would carry out care management functions' (p 6). For many workers, assessment has meant a change in their professional role. Some community nurses, for instance, have noted that increased time spent in care management may mean less time to spend in development work with clients.[31]

In Chapter 5 we look at the 'purchaser–provider split', whereby different functions of planning for and purchasing services are separated from the provision of those services. This aspect of the reforms was meant to ensure that assessment of needs was separated from provision for those needs, but the SSI's early monitoring shows that 'a separation was generally in place for dealing with users with complex needs, but not for those with simpler needs (for example home care, occupational therapy), where assessment was often undertaken by the local authority provider' (*First Impressions*, p 6). Such practice could lead to a continuation of what has been referred to as the 'set list' mentality,[32] which may restrict choice of different types of services, or reduce flexibility of care by using only existing options.

## Assessing means

After the needs assessment and a decision about services to be arranged, there may be an assessment of people's ability to pay for care services. A national system of charging procedures is administered by local authorities for care arranged in a residential or nursing home; local authorities each have their own system of charging for certain local social services. These systems are described more fully on pages 157–164.

An assessment of means is meant to follow the needs assessment, but in some authorities needs assessments are not carried out if people have more than a certain amount of money (for instance, if they have enough to pay for at least a year in a nursing home, or two years in a residential home) (*Implementing Caring for People. Care management*, para 6.14). This does not appear to be strictly in line with local authorities' new duty to assess anyone who appears to them to have a need for a community care service which they may provide. Refusing assessments to people with means could deny them the chance to see whether alternative arrangements could be made, and might mean that certain needs are missed.

# Deciding whether to arrange services to meet needs

It is natural to assume that a 'needs-led' assessment means that the principal goal of the assessment is to meet needs as defined by the user. This is certainly indicated in the quotation from the Summary of the Practice Guidance on page 85, which states that the 'needs and wishes of users' should be 'central to the caring process', and refers to this as a 'needs-led approach'. However, the Policy Guidance shows that the responsibility for deciding which needs are met lies firmly with the local authority. It says that in the assessment account needs to be taken of:

the local authority's criteria for determining what services should be provided [the eligibility criteria];

the types of service they have decided to make available;

the overall range of services provided by other agencies, including health authorities. para 3.15

The Secretary of State for Health has stated that local authorities should 'carry out assessments of individuals with care, and ensure that they do not create commitments that are beyond their means'.[33]

## What is 'need'?

The definition of 'need' depends to some extent on why it is being defined. When individual needs are being assessed, people with apparently the same problem will say that they 'need' different kinds of help, depending on their own circumstances and preferences. 'Need' is sometimes defined differently from 'demand', which is the expressed preference of people who want services or help.

The Practitioners' Guide says that it is 'essential that all care agencies and practitioners share a common understanding of the term "need"' (para 10). In practice this is proving difficult, as the people and organisations involved have different aims and objectives and different ways of working.

The Summary of the Practice Guidance defines need as

the shorthand for the requirements of individuals to enable them to achieve, maintain or restore an acceptable level of social independence or quality of life, as defined by the particular care agency or authority. para 11

The Government's guidance thus places the responsibility for defining the person's needs squarely on the assessor, not on the person involved. It further places the assessor's decisions in the context of the policies of the local authority where he or she works. It states that local authority council members must

revise the policy framework within which managers and practitioners are asked to operate. A needs-led approach requires needs to be explicitly defined and prioritised in policy statements. Elected members ... have to ensure on a continuing basis that they are able to resource the response to the needs for which they accept any responsibility. Summary, para 14

Local authorities are advised to publicise their definition of needs, making clear which they are *required* by law to meet, and which the authority has *discretion* over:

> The more explicit the definition of need, the clearer users and carers will be about their access to services. By and large, local authorities have wider scope for interpreting their responsibilities in law in relation to the care of adults than to the care of children. Summary, para 15

The Practice Guidance goes on to emphasise the personal nature of how people identify their own needs:

> Care management seeks to recognise the individuality of need by challenging practitioners to identify the unique characteristics of each individual's needs and to develop individualised, rather than stereotyped, responses to those needs within the constraints of local policy and resources.
> Summary, para 17

> Ultimately, however, having weighed the views of all parties, including his/her own observation, the assessing practitioner is responsible for defining the user's needs. Practitioners' Guide, para 3.35

This appears to mean that in practice a 'needs-led' approach to assessment and provision of services may not be the same as a 'user-led' approach, a view borne out in a 1993 Audit Commission report (*Taking Care*). Making a clear link between budgets and needs, this report looks at how authorities should set the eligibility criteria with an eye to balancing the books:

> Setting needs eligibility criteria is the most effective way of shaping a coherent approach to need while simultaneously containing expenditure . . . the authority . . . must set criteria to reflect priorities and limit expenditure to the amount budgeted: assessors locally must then operate on a day to day basis entirely within these criteria. para 15

Following the assessment and identification of needs, a decision must be made about what, if any, services the local authority will provide or arrange. There is debate about how needs found in an assessment should be described and recorded, an whether an authority must provide or arrange services once need is identified. The Chief Inspector of the Social Services Inspectorate issued guidance about this in 1992, but the subject remains controversial (see CI (92) 34).

The situation is further complicated by the fact that disabled people must be offered a comprehensive assessment. The Practitioners' Guide states that assessors must understand the 'local authority's interpretation of a disabled person' (para 2.20).

In practice, many local authorities appear not to recognise their duties to disabled people. Only a few authorities' leaflets about the assessment processes mention disabled people's rights to be assessed and to have services provided if they are assessed as needing them. There is little evidence that assessors carry out the duty to assess disabled people, as described on page 80.

There are no hard and fast rules. Different authorities define 'needs' and 'disabled person' in different ways.

## A MATRIX OF NEED AND RISK

Berkshire Social Services Department uses a matrix for people in five client groups, describing different levels of need and risk and putting them into priority order. Each of five major need categories (such as physical safety of the individual or others, or mental health of self or others) is related to a degree of risk to the user if the social services department does not meet some or all of the needs.

There are eight priority levels. Priority 1, for example, is for people whose physical safety is at immediate and high risk, and who cannot be left alone. There may be no carer present, or the carer may be unable or unwilling to provide support. Priority 3 is assigned where a high level of support is required every day, or there may be a risk of physical harm. A carer may be showing signs of stress. Priority 5 is allocated to people who have a significantly reduced quality of life owing to limited daily living skills. This could include people who need help perhaps once a week, and who have no social contact outside the immediate family or neighbours. Priority 8 covers people who have 'an intermittent inability to enjoy full social contact'.

People likely to be in priorities 1 to 3 will have a full assessment of need; they are guaranteed services if they are assessed as needing them. People likely to be in priorities 4 to 8 will also have an assessment of need, but the assessment process may be shorter (unless a higher level need is shown). Particular levels of service are not guaranteed to people in these groups, but the authority has set aside some money for preventive services.[34]

These are just some examples of how Berkshire is tackling the task of defining who is eligible for services – *after* the assessment is carried out, in line with the Government's policy that services should be targeted on those in greatest need, and within the limits of available resources.

Users, carers and policy-makers may well have very different views about the success of the new assessment process. Thinking back to the objectives of the reforms, described in Chapter 2, we can see that the Audit Commission and the Practice Guidance focus on the need to 'target' services on those with the greatest needs (Key Objective 1) and to assess individual need, 'design care arrangements' and make provision 'within available resources' (Key Change 1). Thus, taking account of the views of users and carers, often referred to as a 'needs-led' approach, is to take place within the framework of available resources.

Policy-makers may well judge the new system to be a success if it has defined needs and eligibility for services according to tight eligibility criteria. However, people who feel they need some form of support, but who do not come within these criteria, may feel that the new system is not a success as far as they are concerned.

For instance, debate is increasing about the relationship between meeting needs and the cost of different options for care. This could create a new paradox in the reformed system, which aims to 'target' resources on those most in need. Many of these people will need the most expensive arrangements for care at home. These may well cost more than a place in a care home. The pressure to keep costs down might mean that some such people can no longer be offered the option of staying at home.

## The care plan

The assessment procedure is part of the process of care management, which involves in addition the setting up and carrying out of a care plan (where it is agreed that services will be provided), monitoring how it is working, and reviewing the assessment regularly. A care plan should include objectives for service provision which are agreed with service users and carers. In practice many care plans are simply statements about how much service will be provided, or what time people will call. Indeed, many service users are not given care plans or, indeed, written statements of the outcome of their 'assessment'.

Where people have very complex needs, or need very high levels of services, their care may be arranged by 'care managers'. There is no set pattern for how care management is organised. In some authorities, care managers assess people's needs, help to work out a care plan, and monitor and review how the process is working, but are not responsible for managing budgets for services. In other areas, care managers will have special budgets for particular kinds of care. These are called 'devolved budgets' because they are moved away from the central administration of the authority. The idea is that the person who is closest to the service user is able to make decisions about what kind of help is most appropriate, within the limits of that manager's budget. Such budgets are generally used to help people remain in their present home, and, as we have seen, may be set at an amount per person around the cost of a place in a care home. Devolved budgets are seen by many as a key to arranging more flexible and individualised services.

**Mr O'Malley** has tripped on the sill of the back door and fractured his hip. He is in hospital recovering, learning to walk with a frame, and contemplating returning home.

His family live 200 miles away. They are concerned that he might fall again and feel guilty that they can't visit more frequently. They feel he might be safer in a care home.

But Mr O'Malley is determined to remain at home, if necessary moving the bed downstairs. An assessment is arranged in the hospital, to sort out his care needs. The social worker, physiotherapist, occupational therapist and family doctor all agree on the services which will help him remain at home, and a care manager takes responsibility for arranging this support and paying for some of it.

An arrangement is made with a neighbour to shop and do other errands for him. Mr O'Malley will contribute to the cost of this service. A home from hospital scheme will help with other care in the first few weeks. A physiotherapist and the home gardening service will also offer support.

From time to time Mr O'Malley's 'care package' will be reassessed. If his needs have changed or increased, he and the care manager may need to readjust it.

Mr O'Malley reassures his family that he would rather be at slight risk of another fall than move to a care home, away from his friends and neighbours.

Not everyone has a 'care manager'. As we have seen, local authorities have set up their assessment and care management services in many different ways. Where care managers exist, they may carry out some or all assessments; they may also offer ongoing support to people with the most complicated needs. However, the term care *management* (as distinct from care *manager*) simply describes the process of assessment and planning and review which should be part of all good practice. People without care managers should know who has the major responsibility for their care and can serve as a link with other providers.

## The care programme approach

There is a special 'care programme' approach for people who are patients of a consultant psychiatrist, including people with dementia. This is described in Circular HC(90)23/LASSL(90)11. The aim is to ensure assessment and reassessment of people being treated in the community, and a formal discharge plan for every patient discharged from psychiatric hospital. Patients and their carers should be closely involved in preparing care programmes, which should involve the cooperation of various professionals such as nurses, psychologists, GPs and social workers. If a lack of resources prevents a patient's minimum needs for treatment being met in the community – in terms of both continuing health care and any necessary social care – inpatient treatment should be offered or continued.

The care programme approach is at the heart of one of the main aims of community care: the replacement of large, institutionalised hospitals by locally based care either in ordinary housing or in various forms of sheltered or supervised housing. The approach has not been adopted everywhere, although health authorities were due to do so by April 1991. There is concern in many areas that hospitals for people with mental health problems are closing before adequate community facilities are available for people being discharged. Yet some people feel the resettlement programme is being carried out far too slowly. There is a dilemma between the desire to move people out of large institutions into smaller homes and the fear that such a move may mean greater isolation, and perhaps neglect, if there are not enough resources in the community to provide appropriate support.

From April 1993 fundholding GPs assumed responsibility for a comprehensive mental health outpatient and community service. National Health Service guidance (EL(92)48) states:

> where a fundholder purchases psychiatric services from an NHS unit or Trust, the contractual arrangement should require these organisations to operate fully the Care Programme Approach. para 8.16

As we have seen (p 25), community care for people with mental health problems has been the subject of much concern. In 1993 the Secretary of State for Health announced a ten-point plan to improve care for people with mental health problems who have been in contact with the specialist mental health services, including proposals for supervision registers and supervised discharge for certain patients who might be at risk, or cause risk to others. In 1994, strengthened guidance was issued on the care programme approach and on responsibilities for after care under section 117 of the Mental Health Act (LASSL(94)4/HSG(94)27 – see p 196).

Different models of care management may be seen as appropriate for different situations. Work is needed to sort out the overlap, for instance between care management by social services departments and the care programme approach, which is largely the responsibility of the health service. Yet concern remains, and focuses on the need for a more integrated national policy for people with mental health problems – taking into account housing, health, social services and benefits.[35] Similar comments

## DECISION-MAKING FOR MENTALLY INCAPACITATED PEOPLE

Many people who need community care services are not able to make decisions for themselves. They may have mental illnesses such as dementia, or learning disabilities, or have suffered brain damage through an accident or stroke.

We do not have a good framework for making decisions for such people. The National Assistance Act 1948 gives powers to detain people for their own or others' safety. Guardianship powers exist under the Mental Health Act 1983 for a guardian to make certain decisions about a person's welfare, but these are rarely used. Powers of attorney or receivership under the Court of Protection cover people's financial affairs but they do not cover personal decisions.

As part of the assessment and care management process, decisions often have to be made about whether people should be cared for at home or in a care home or hospital. Some people neglect themselves at home, yet are resistant to being helped.

Advocacy schemes as described on page 86 can help represent the views of mentally incapacitated people, but such schemes have no legal status and are not uniformly available. Sections of the Disabled Persons Act 1986 which formalise the role of advocates or representatives have not been implemented.

The ACE Books publication *The Law and Vulnerable Elderly People* (details on p 211) looks at the many issues involved, as do discussion reports from the Law Commission on mentally incapacitated adults and decision-making. Work is continuing to try to develop a way of making decisions for such people that fully protects their interests.

have been made by Age Concern and others about community care policies in general.

## Reviewing the assessment

There may be differences of opinion about how the assessor defines or prioritises a person's needs. Part of the Disabled Persons Act which has not been implemented says that people should be able to have a review of their assessment under that Act. Some have argued that people should be able to appeal if they are not happy about the assessment and its outcome under the 1990 Act. However, the Policy Guidance states that:

> Decisions on service provision should be reached in discussion with users and carers and every effort should be made to ensure that the result is acceptable to them. A formal judicial appeal procedure would be foreign to such arrangements and it would not be appropriate to introduce one.
>
> para 3.54

The first step for people wishing to obtain a review of their community care assessment will thus be through the *complaints procedure*, which social services departments must have (see Chapter 6). People should be told about this procedure when their needs are being assessed, but the extent to which this happens in practice is not clear.

If, however, people feel that they are not being helped appropriately under the various relevant Acts, they can seek redress through the courts; they can also appeal to the Local Government Ombudsman if they feel the authority has not acted properly (see p 130 for further details).

# DILEMMAS OF ASSESSMENT

## Assessment as rationing

Assessment should be a way of getting close to people's own views about what services they need. However, it can also be a way of weeding out people, to see whom the local authority will arrange services for and who does not come high enough up the list. It is a way of 'rationing' services.

As we have seen, there is a tension between the idea of 'user-led' assessment and the 'targeting' of resources on people in greatest need. Some social services departments are worried about the assessment process raising expectations which cannot be met. The demand for assessments is growing. There is evidence that some assessments do not reflect people's *actual* needs, but only the needs they are allowed to express in line with those the authority feels able to meet. Such a system suppresses any understanding of the true level of need, unless the unmet needs are carefully recorded and fed back into the planning system.

In general, legislation about health and personal social services is interpreted as requiring authorities to do things *within the limits of available resources*. This is the broad framework within which the Government has based the community care reforms. This means that it is difficult to define exactly how a particular need – or how many needs – should be met by public provision. Similarly, it is difficult for people to judge whether *their* authority arranges enough of a particular service or makes available a wide enough range of services. In late 1994, some authorities urged the Government to make more resources available to meet growing need. Among others, Gloucestershire and the Isle of Wight had to take steps to revise eligibility criteria and limit access to services as their community care funds ran low (see Chapter 8).

The Acts of Parliament described earlier in this chapter create *duties* for local authorities, but they are rarely formally challenged over them. Frail and vulnerable people are often not in a position to press for their needs to be met when they are told that nothing is possible. Many people thought that the 1990 Act, and the new assessment procedures, would lead to formal challenges through the courts and judicial review if people believed that local authorities were not meeting their statutory duties. To date only a few such challenges have taken place (see p 131). Chapter 6 discusses more fully how individuals can challenge local authorities when they feel their specific needs are not being met.

In addition to its rationing function, the assessment process may also be seen as a way of giving power in various ways to service users or potential users and their carers. For instance, if they are assessed as having needs which the authority then says it cannot meet, at least they then have knowledge which they can use to campaign for more or better services, or for more public funds to be spent on people with community care needs. This rather optimistic view depends on older people and their carers being included in a true partnership in the assessment process, but this does not always happen.

More broadly, assessments could empower service users by ensuring that evidence of unmet need is fed back into the planning process. However, this aspect of the reforms proved problematic in the early days, as many authorities were reluctant to record formally evidence of needs which they could not meet, for fear of legal challenges that they were not meeting their statutory duties. This situation may be changing, as authorities develop more sophisticated information systems, and as different ways of recording needs and outcomes are developed. Indeed, some authorities have said that they would welcome legal challenges to clarify the law.

## Acceptable risk

Assessment often reveals the difficulties of achieving a balance between allowing people to take risks and protecting individuals, their carers and other people. Professionals' views of 'acceptable' risk may not be the same as those of the individual, family or neighbours. Conflicts often arise, for instance, in judging what is 'acceptable' independence for someone who constantly leaves the gas on, thereby threatening the welfare of neighbours. The person concerned may refuse all assistance.

The use of the matrix described on page 93 will relate as much to the level of available resources as to any absolute judgement about reasonable levels of risk. Making public the criteria for allocation of priorities should ideally empower service users, carers and other interested parties to raise the issue through the political process, if they feel that changes are needed to the system.

Judgements about risk are closely linked with 'choice' for service users.

## Choice

The community care reforms are rooted in the idea that people should have choice about how their care needs are met. Assessment should be user-led, but it gives the ultimate responsibility for defining need and working out how or if it is met to the local authority through the assessor or care manager. How much choice the user has will depend on many things, such as how much information the user has about available services; the resources the local authority has available; and the priorities that it has determined. For instance, many authorities effectively deny users with low-level needs the positive choice to opt for care in a care home, which lies well down the 'preferred options' for places of care. The amount of 'choice' available to a person needing to be protected, perhaps because they suffer from dementia, will depend on a fine balance in judging the amount of acceptable risk and the safety of the person or others.

## THE DIRECTION ON CHOICE

The reforms have included a new element of choice for people assessed as needing residential or nursing home care. A Direction from the Secretary of State for Health requires local authorities to arrange a place in the home of a person's choice in England and Wales (and, by arrangement, in Scotland), provided that certain conditions are met. These are that:

- a place is available, and the home is willing to arrange a contract according to the local authority's terms and conditions;
- the place is suitable for the person's assessed needs;
- the place does not cost more than the authority would 'usually' expect to pay for someone with the same assessed needs.

Where the place does cost more than the authority would 'usually' pay to meet the person's assessed needs, a 'third party' can make a contribution, as is discussed on pages 159–160. Circulars LAC(92)27 and LAC(93)18 give local authorities considerable detail about how the Direction on Choice should be carried out.

In many areas, the Direction on Choice has meant that people are offered full information about the options open to them in choosing a home. In other areas, there has been misunderstanding about the extent to which choice can be offered, often related to the amount of money which the authority is willing to pay, for instance for a 'more expensive' home which is nearer to the resident's spouse or other relatives and which, arguably, is essential to meet that person's 'assessed needs'.

Guidance on long-term care issued in 1995 (see p 173) states that if a place in a particular home of choice is not available at the time of discharge, and is not likely to be available in the near future, it may be necessary for the patient to be discharged to another home until a place becomes available (HSG(95)8, para 26).

As we discuss in Chapter 5, the 'Choice' Direction does not apply to people in respect of care in their own homes, although guidance on care management and assessment stresses the importance of choice for service users and carers.

It should also be remembered that 'choice' for users of community care may be severely restricted because of their illness or disability. In general, people have not 'chosen' to be in the position of requiring care, so frequently the choices available to them are options for improving a situation they would not have chosen. Many studies have shown that users of services often feel that they are given little or no choice when decisions are made about their care.

The reforms have, however, allowed services to develop to give many people the choice of staying at home where this would not have existed before. In one authority a voluntary organisation provides an intensive home care service. This is provided as part of a 'care package' which the local authority purchases – up to a maximum limit of expenditure per week, roughly the cost of a place in a care home. The problem with such packages is that they may well not offer some people *enough* service to give them a real choice of staying at home.

**A care worker:** 'Within these costs, we can start with the basics and then provide, say, three overnights. So you *know* they're not getting full care, but they *are* getting community care. For some this is a great improvement, and a lot of these people would not previously have had the choice of remaining at home.'

##  Negative views of the assessment process

Assessment should be a positive process to find out as much as possible about a person's needs for care. However, if the assessment is seen as a hurdle to be got over, many people will be discouraged from approaching the authority for help. It may be quite difficult to overcome their diffidence, which might arise because:

- People may not understand how the procedure works.
- There may be no interpreting service to help people whose first language is not English, or who are deaf.
- People may not want their financial means to be assessed.
- Disablement benefits have to be put towards services offered, when there is already difficulty making ends meet.

All these problems and others have been identified in the new system.

Assessment and the process of care management should be used by the local authority within a framework of objectives and priorities to examine the needs of individuals, and then to decide which if any of these needs can be met by provision of services.

Many of the aims of the assessment and care management process have been slow to develop – which is understandable when we consider the major changes which have taken place. Early experience shows:

- The volume of enquiries and referrals has increased dramatically following the introduction of the reforms.

- Users and assessors are not generally agreeing objectives for care following the assessment.

- Financial assessments are complicated and difficult to administer – some staff dislike having to do them. In addition, charges for non-residential social services are increasingly unpopular with users and carers.

- Involvement of health personnel is patchy – and in many areas GPs are hardly involved at all.

- There is little evidence of local authorities using information from assessments for their future planning.

For some people – particularly those with complex needs – innovative (and often expensive) care packages have been arranged. Some older people, however, may not be so fortunate. In some areas, as we have seen, complex needs that would be expensive to meet may simply result in pressure to move to a residential or nursing home – particularly where night-time care or care at weekends is needed.

After initial problems, authorities are increasingly setting up systems to record unmet need. Reviews of assessments and monitoring of service provision should also be important in showing how users feel about the services they are receiving and indicating where there are gaps.

What is not clear is on whose terms the overall success of the system is to be judged: policy-makers and administrators often focus on tailoring needs to resources, while users and carers focus on their own experiences and perceptions of need, and their rights to assessments and certain services.

# 5 Purchasing and Contracting

Before the full implementation of the community care reforms in 1993, and the National Health Service reorganisation in 1991, most public health and social services were planned for and provided by public authorities. This was called 'direct service provision'. For instance, District Health Authorities operated hospitals and community health services. Social services departments ran their own residential homes – 'Part III homes' – and had their own home help services and day centres.

There were exceptions to this general rule. In some areas, voluntary organisations ran some services by arrangement with the local authority. For instance, the Women's Royal Voluntary Service has long provided meals on wheels on behalf of social services authorities. Many Age Concern organisations have been major providers of day care and other services. These would frequently have been run under formal arrangements and would have received financial help from the local authority in the form of a grant to help them provide the service.

## LOCAL AUTHORITIES AS ENABLERS

The community care and health service reforms aimed to change the role of authorities which were previously mainly *providers* to that of *enablers*. As enablers, the local authorities have a number of tasks which we talk about in this chapter. The Department of Health's Practice Guidance on purchasing and contracting describes the 'enabling' role of the local authority with respect to community care:

to identify the needs for care among the population it serves, plan how best to meet those needs, set overall strategies, priorities and targets, commission and purchase as well as provide necessary services and ensure their quality and value.                                    *Purchase of Service*, para 4.3

This role thus involves many of the planning activities which we looked at in Chapter 3. It also involves assessment and care management, as these are necessary if the local authority is to know what services it should purchase or provide.

# The White Paper

The change to an 'enabling' role is said by the Government to offer more choice of services; to provide services which meet individual needs in a more flexible and innovative way; and to encourage competition between providers, resulting in better value for money and a more cost-effective service (*Caring for People*, para 3.4.3).

The White Paper also said:

> The Government will expect local authorities to make use wherever possible of services from voluntary, 'not for profit' and private providers insofar as this represents a cost effective care choice. Social services authorities will continue to play a valuable role in the provision of services, but in those cases where they are still the main or sole providers of services, they will be expected to take all reasonable steps to secure diversity of provision.
>
> para 3.4.1

Social services authorities still have to make sure that certain people have access to services if they need them: they have *statutory duties*, as we saw in Chapter 2 (p 52). But instead of providing most of these services themselves, the Government wants them increasingly to *arrange* services offered by a variety of *providers*. The providers can include the local authorities themselves, but also private, voluntary and other bodies. Authorities are thus encouraged to promote the development of independent sector provision – to develop what is called a 'mixed economy of care'.

This should not mean the end of 'council services'. The Government sees a continuing role for local authority direct provision, in particular for very dependent people or those with 'challenging behaviour', or where there are no other suitable forms of provision (*Caring for People*, para 3.4.11). In addition, the Government's Circular LAC(93)10 also states the

Department of Health's view that because of their duties under section 21 of the National Assistance Act 1948 (as amended by section 1 of the Community Care (Residential Accommodation) Act 1992) authorities will have to 'make some direct provision for residential care under Part III of the 1948 Act'. However, some councils which are proud of the services they run are increasingly being encouraged by the Government to transfer some of these services to other providers, and to stimulate independent provision in place of their own. This involves 'managing the market', as we saw in Chapter 3.

In the first two years of the funding transfer, local authorities in England have been required to spend at least 85 per cent of the 'transfer element' of the Special Transitional Grant (see pp 165–167) on community care services provided independently of the local authorities. This requirement will continue in 1995–96.

---

### THE INDEPENDENT SECTOR

For the purposes of community care plans and the '85 per cent rule', the independent sector is defined in Circular LAC(94)12 as

*. . . individuals who are not employed by any local authority under a contract of service or organisations which are not owned, controlled or managed by any local authority or more than one authority. It includes both private and voluntary providers.*

*This definition includes such providers as NHS trusts, which are not generally considered as part of the 'independent sector' in this book, as they are statutory organisations.*

---

In their community care plans, local authorities are expected to show how they will stimulate the independent sector to provide community care services:

Social services authorities will be expected to make clear in their community care plans what steps they will be taking to make increased use of non-statutory service providers or, where such providers are not currently available, how they propose to stimulate such activity. *Caring for People*, para 3.4.5

The White Paper suggested they do this by:

- devising specifications of service requirements and arrangements for tenders and contracts;

- stimulating the setting up of 'not-for-profit' agencies;

- identifying self-contained areas of their own work which can be 'floated off' as self-managing units;

- stimulating the development of new voluntary sector activity (*Caring for People*, para 3.4.6).

These suggestions have been taken up by local authorities in a variety of ways. Most local authorities have now produced specifications for domiciliary care, and are inviting providers to go on their register of providers or to tender for contracts. Some authorities have helped new independent organisations with the cost of preparing business plans for taking over certain services. In 1992, under a special 'Caring for People at Home' initiative, new money was provided by the Government for local authorities to give to independent sector providers to develop new community care schemes.

We saw in Chapter 3 that local authorities must show in their plans how they plan to use the independent sector in future.

# The 'purchaser–provider split'

The emphasis on purchasing and contracting and moves towards systems of assessment and care management have led many authorities to change their structures. They have divided tasks which were formerly carried out by the same people, or within the same section of the department. For instance, the home care organiser has traditionally been responsible for assessing people's needs *and* managing the service. In many authorities these responsibilities have now been split. One part of the department is responsible for assessing needs and arranging to *purchase* the necessary service from a *provider* – either another part of the department or an outside organisation.

Where this has meant reorganising a social services department into divisions or units with these separate responsibilities, it is often referred to as the 'purchaser–provider split'. Major changes in working patterns have thus occurred in some local authorities.

In some areas these changes have created considerable pressure on staff and some confusion to service users. Such changes will continue as many authorities look for better ways of working, and with the upheaval of local government reorganisation in many areas.

## THE PURCHASER–PROVIDER SPLIT WITHIN THE HEALTH SERVICE

Health authorities were required to introduce a purchase–provider split in 1991. They are responsible for assessing the needs of their local populations and purchasing services to meet these needs within available resources. Nearly all services are now run by separate NHS trusts.

A paradox of the reforms is that GP fundholders are increasingly major purchasers, but remain providers as well. They are, for instance, responsible for community nursing and for outpatient mental health services. They purchase such services for their patients while continuing to provide the general medical services for which all GPs are responsible. In this way, the fairly clear-cut purchaser–provider split which has been implemented between health authorities and NHS trusts has been made less clear by the transfer of purchasing to increasing numbers of GP fundholders.

Some authorities have transferred services – particularly residential homes, day care and home helps – to specially created organisations. There are several types of 'not-for-profit' companies, or 'trusts', which have been developed to take on services, for example in Cheshire, Somerset and Tameside.

**Tameside** is a metropolitan borough near Manchester. It has transferred all its homes for older people to an independent organisation which is able to raise money on the open market to pay for improvements to the homes. Local authorities cannot freely raise money, as the amount they can raise for capital expenditure has to be approved each year by central government.

Because Tameside no longer has any residential homes of its own for older people, it is no longer a 'direct provider' of residential care. However, it still has a statutory duty under the National Assistance Act 1948 to provide residential care for people who need it and for whom it is not otherwise available. Tameside must therefore *arrange* places for older people as needed. It can do this either in its former homes or in other independent homes.

In doing this, Tameside assesses a resident's means to see how much they should pay for care, similarly to how it would have done if the person had lived in one of Tameside's homes before the transfer, using the charging procedures described on pages 157–161.

In the jargon of the community care reforms, Tameside is a 'purchaser' of residential care: it arranges such care through contracts.

### Arranging residential and nursing home care

The community care reforms extended local authorities' responsibility for arranging care by adding responsibility for arranging care for people needing continuing nursing care. The transfer of funds from the DSS to local authorities particularly affected the purchasing and contracting responsibilities of local authorities, which are responsible for arranging publicly funded residential home care and social care for people at home, and much publicly funded nursing home care. The priorities they choose determine the kinds of care which will be available for people whom they assess as having needs which they will support. Health authorities may also have responsibilities to provide continuing care (see pp 172–174).

# CONTRACTS

The Government has said that their bargaining power should enable local authorities to obtain good quality care from care homes or home care agencies at the most economic price – a principal goal of the community care reforms. Contracts with outside organisations are legally binding, whereas no such contract exists when services are purchased from provider units within the authority. Such internal arrangements are often referred to as 'service-level agreements', although many authorities also use this term for some external contracts, particularly those which replace grants to voluntary organisations.

## Types of contract

Different words and phrases are used to described contracts. Here are some general descriptions:

**Block contracts** are used to buy a certain amount of service for a set amount of money (for example all the places at a day centre). Such contracts guarantee income for the provider, but they could involve the authority paying for services not actually used. Block contracts could reduce choice for users, for instance if there is only one organisation providing all day care for older people.

**Spot contracts** involve purchasing units of services (for instance a bed in a residential home or so many hours of domestic care for a person) as and when the authority needs them. Spot contracts do not guarantee business for the provider, and allow the authority to pay for only what it needs. Users may have more choice, although this will not apply if one organisation is awarded a tender to provide all spot contracts. How much choice is available may also depend on which organisations can offer the services needed at the time.

**Cost-and-volume contracts** are a compromise between the two: the authority pays something towards the provider's costs, or guarantees to buy a minimum amount of service. The authority then buys additional units of services as needed. This type of contract is used when a provider needs some security of income, for instance a voluntary group running day care, for which the authority is the only purchaser.

Spot contracts came into widespread use from April 1993 to buy residential and nursing home care. For non-residential care, authorities are increasingly following a pattern of listing or accrediting providers, agreeing standard contract conditions, and then purchasing services with spot contracts.

## Contract specifications

Local authorities can set out in a contract exactly what they want from a particular service. Setting out specifications – and monitoring them – should be an important way of promoting quality. Self-monitoring is increasingly seen as part of quality assurance:

**A social services officer:** 'We are increasingly seeing part of the task of monitoring as the job of the service providers themselves. We expect them as part of their contract to carry out a review of the client's position after a month. Our staff will carry out random checks of these reviews.'

We look again at quality assurance in Chapter 7.

According to the Government's Policy Guidance, users should be involved in drawing up service specifications. The views of users and carers should be taken into account. Local representative organisations, such as charities, may play an important role in speaking on behalf of people with different needs. Users' views of services should be fed back into the contracting process when the contract is due for renewal.

Service specifications may include details of the service, the quality and quantity of the service, and how these will be monitored. A service specification can be a very long document. If a local authority has made a contract with a voluntary organisation like Age Concern to provide day care, both organisations want to be sure that they have covered all aspects of the service in the specification. After all, very large sums of money are involved, and it is vitally important to make sure that the quality of the service is good.

In some areas, care home owners have challenged the service specifications which local authorities have imposed as conditions for homes to be considered as 'approved' providers. The homes argued that the fact that they were registered should be sufficient for them to be 'approved', and said that the local authorities were making unreasonable demands on them. Judgements have depended on the circumstances in different areas, but they have shown that in many cases local authorities are free to impose certain criteria on care home owners that wish to provide contracted places to the local authority.[36]

## WHAT CONTRACTS SHOULD COVER

The Practice Guidance on contracting describes what contracts should cover, including:

- the length of the contract (whether for a fixed period or renewable);
- what is being bought;
- how changes in the contract will be handled;
- the procedure for resolving disputes;
- default arrangements;
- insurance;
- complaints procedures for users and carers;
- the review procedure.

The Practice Guidance says that social services departments should use race relations and equal opportunities laws to ensure their contracting processes 'do not discriminate against women, people with disabilities or people from minority ethnic groups or their organisations' (*Purchase of Service*, paras 4.3.8–4.3.9).

# Whom are the contracts with?

In some areas of local government – for instance in refuse collection – local authorities have been required to put services out to tender, so that their own services and private services have had to compete for the contract. In the case of social services, however, they do not *have* to do this, although the requirement in England that authorities spend 85 per cent of the transfer element of the Special Transitional Grant (see pp 165–166) on independent sector provision has stimulated moves to buy services from external providers (including services that were formerly part of local authority provision, as we saw on p 108).

Councils may put some services out to tender, or they may negotiate with private, voluntary or 'not-for-profit' organisations to see whether they would like to provide services under contract to the council. Here we look at some issues of contracting with the voluntary and the private sectors.

# Contracting with the voluntary sector

As we have already seen, some voluntary organisations have been providing services for many years. They have traditionally received grants from local authorities in recognition of the work they do, but not necessarily tied to a particular service or activity. There is now a move towards contracting – towards a 'contract culture', as it is sometimes described. Many local authorities are trying to distinguish between using grants for short-term work, or where small sums of money are involved, and introducing contracts for long-term funding or more substantial payments. Some authorities are linking agreement on contracts with continuation of general grants, a cause of some concern to voluntary organisations which do not wish to go down the 'contracting' road. Many local authorities have changed their attitude towards voluntary organisations whose services they may have grant-supported for many years.

**A chief officer of a voluntary organisation:** 'We've got contracts for services with the borough, and get a grant towards core costs – things like my salary. Now they want to make a contract for this as well. I'm worried that it's a way of them making sure that we do what they want – not necessarily what we, as a charity, think we should do.'

This example illustrates a dilemma for some voluntary organisations which may not wish to change or expand their role, but which are dependent on local authority funding for some or all of their work. Although some voluntary organisations have been major service providers for years, others are now being encouraged to follow this route, funded through formal contracts or service agreements rather than by the less formal grant arrangements of previous years.

## THE ROLES OF VOLUNTARY ORGANISATIONS

Sir Roy Griffiths summarised the varied roles of voluntary sector organisations – in addition to providing services:

*self-help;*

*information provision;*

*befriending;*

*advocacy;*

*public education;*

*campaigning;*

*innovating and monitoring.*                    Griffiths Report, para 8.11

If voluntary organisations are increasingly expected to contribute to the 'mixed economy of care' by becoming service providers, there are some worries that their ability to act as independent observers of public policies and innovators of new types of care may be reduced. If they have a large contract with the local authority to provide one service, will they be able to comment on some other aspect of the local authority's policy without endangering the contract on which they depend? If they must follow the local authority's priorities in order to obtain a contract, they may have to neglect innovatory or less high priority schemes which may have been the main reason why they were set up in the first place, or to neglect people whom they would previously have wanted to support.

There are other concerns about voluntary organisations and contracting. Contracting is a complicated process, involving legal responsibilities on both sides. Some small organisations have neither the expertise nor the resources to deal with this. They are worried that they might be overlooked completely if authorities tend to turn to larger organisations to contract services, perhaps reducing or cutting altogether their grants to other organisations. This has already happened in some areas.

Increasingly local authorities are dealing only with contractors whom they 'accredit' – that is, those who give evidence of their integrity, financial stability and ability to meet quality standards. The extensive form-filling, and sometimes the fees involved, can prove daunting – or impossible – for some smaller organisations.

Most (but not all) services provided by voluntary organisations rely on volunteer help. Some concern has been expressed about the ability of such services to contract for tight specifications, when they depend on volunteers. The contract specifications may also require levels of training and systems of control which volunteers do not wish to undertake.

These problems all relate to the nature of voluntary organisations themselves. As time passes and contracting increases, the nature of some of these organisations may change even more than it already has.

# Contracting with the private sector

Local authorities are also being encouraged to expand the range of services for which they contract through the private sector. Private care home provision has grown dramatically, partly fuelled before 1993 by the availability of special rates of Income Support. There is also a growing sector of private home care providers, although local authorities and some voluntary organisations have traditionally been the major source of help at home.

In some areas private sector providers believe that the local authority is reluctant to contract with them. As we have seen, a legal obligation has been created for local authorities to consult with independent sector providers in preparing community care plans, and to show how they plan to use the independent sector in purchasing services.

In many areas the distribution of services is uneven – in some coastal areas, for example, there is an abundance of care homes, while in some inner cities or rural areas, there are few or none. One aim of the mixed economy of care is that services should be attracted to areas where they have previously been underprovided. However, the transfer of DSS funds to local authorities in the first year to some extent reinforced the unevenness in distribution of care homes, although the system changed unexpectedly in 1994 (see pp 167–168).

Information has been published for care homes to help them diversify into other areas, such as providing services in people's own homes.[37] Such diversification may help some providers to develop their business as the number of people entering homes goes down – as it is in many areas. Local authorities also need to make plans for arranging care for residents when care homes close, as many inevitably will do.

The private sector is becoming well established in some areas as a provider of domiciliary care. Although there are a few large organisations in the field, most private agencies are relatively small businesses, which can often provide flexible care, covering long or difficult hours. However, they may face similar problems to those of small voluntary organisations in coping with often complex contracting procedures, and they may be undercut by large providers. Particularly where contracts are awarded by tender to a single provider, the bigger organisation is likely to have a price advantage. This could result in the market becoming dominated by a few companies, with a possible reduction in variety and user choice.

There is another challenge with domiciliary care. Often the most individualised, flexible care package will involve an individual, or several very local people, in providing small amounts of care at regular – or perhaps irregular – intervals. As we see later in discussing the Independent Living Fund, the employment of such people can be quite complex, either for the local authority or for individuals. It is perhaps this type of very flexible, locally provided, individual care which is most in need of 'devolved budgets', whereby care managers can make specific, individual arrangements. Ultimately, many people would prefer to be given the money and to make the arrangements themselves (see p 118).

A brief look at contracting with the private and voluntary sectors may be in as much danger of overgeneralising as we are when we refer to members of 'client groups', as discussed in Chapter 1 (pp 21–24). Organisations and businesses in both sectors feel they have a lot to offer to community care, yet also wish to guard their individuality and special contribution to the overall pattern of care. Many are reliant on public funds and on their relationships with local authorities and – importantly – health authorities. In thinking about the 'mixed economy of care' it is important not to fall into the trap of thinking that all or even most of a particular 'sector' is the same. Small private sector providers may have more in common with smaller voluntary organisations than with large-scale companies.

## Monitoring contracts

The Practice Guidance on purchasing describes a number of possibilities for monitoring how well contracts are working (*Purchase of Service*, para 5.6):

- The contract manager should 'monitor the quality of services offered as part of the contract management function'.

- In the case of residential homes, the inspection unit may be asked to carry out evaluations of contract compliance, in addition to its statutory inspection duties. (However, the inspection unit, as part of the authority which also provides care, may not be seen as an impartial judge of how contracts are working.)

- Care management staff gather evidence and develop views about services, and receive feedback from service users.

- The formal complaints procedure and user satisfaction surveys should provide useful information; with vulnerable clients, 'the views of advocates should be sought'.

The Practice Guidance also says:

> Information systems must be capable of handling information on quality if it is to become a routine part of the management process. Most performance indicators relate to quantity and cost, thus providing a skewed view of services if taken on their own.　　　　　　　　　　　para 5.6.5

Monitoring is one of the most talked about parts of the community care reforms; it affects nearly every aspect, but is very difficult to do. There is a danger with contracts that they will specify items which are easy to quantify – such as number of staff and hours of care – but will have difficulty in identifying how quality can be checked on. In Chapter 7 we look in more detail at quality and standard-setting. In general, users and carers have to date had little impact on contract specification and monitoring. Most information systems are not able to deal with the complex task of relating needs to planning and purchasing.

# SOME IMPLICATIONS OF CONTRACTING FOR SERVICE USERS

## Choice

We saw at the beginning of this chapter that the introduction of the 'mixed economy of care' and the 'purchaser–provider split' was meant to encourage more choice for users of services.

For residential and nursing homes, we have seen that the Government has placed a legal duty on local authorities to arrange a place in the home of a person's choice (see p 101).

For day and domiciliary care services, however, there is no legal requirement to offer choice in this way. We have already seen that different types of contract can affect the amount of choice which users have (see pp 109–110). Even where there are a number of accredited providers, in some cases the aim is simply to purchase the lowest-cost option, thus negating choice. In general, bearing in mind the necessity to match needs and resources, the authority will purchase the amount of care which assessors think is needed – or which matches the resources available and falls within the defined eligibility criteria. Anything over and above this will have to be paid for as an 'extra'. In practice, choice (both of residential and non-residential services) may benefit most those who are able to pay extra fees and, indeed, who are able and willing to express their own views.

## Consumer power

When we enter into a contract, we have rights as consumers. We pay for a service or a product, and if that product is not fit for use or the service is not satisfactory, we are protected under consumer legislation on the sale of goods and services.

Consumers' rights with respect to contracted community care services do not work in quite the same way. In care homes, for instance, the local authority is legally responsible for paying the fees where it has arranged the place. This means that the local authority purchases the place and pays the bill, and collects as much as it can from the resident, according to a formula laid down by the Government (see pp 158–159). Unless a special arrangement has been made, the resident does not have a direct contractual relationship with the care home (see pp 119–120).

The same is true for services provided in people's homes or in day centres. If the person is paying for the service directly, he or she can withdraw from the arrangement if the service is not satisfactory. If the person is using a service which has been purchased by the local authority on his or her behalf, the contract is then between the local authority and the provider – and possibly between the local authority and the user. The user does not have the power of the purse-strings to influence the service provider.

This means that the process of contract specification and monitoring is very important to the user. If users' views cannot influence both the drawing up of specifications and the checking to see that these are met, the user's voice may be lost. In most cases the older user has very little purchasing power: it is always possible to end the arrangement, but since the user is dependent on the local authority for making the arrangement, and presumably cannot do without the service, his or her negotiating power may be very limited. As we note in Chapter 7, many people are reluctant to 'rock the boat'.

Some organisations of and for disabled people argue that the only way to give service users real choice and autonomy is to provide the money for them to purchase their own services. In many authorities, there are arrangements to pool some funds, perhaps using a voluntary agency to do so. This means that some people can make their own care management arrangements, using so-called 'indirect' payment schemes. There is evidence that disabled people who arrange their own services through such payment schemes feel they have more choice and control, and more reliable services.[38]

With the exception of the Independent Living Fund, the law does not give social services departments in England the power to give money directly to adults, although it can be done in Scotland. However, the Secretary of State for Health has announced plans to introduce legislation in 1995–96 to permit direct payments to disabled people.[39] If such payments are introduced, more work will be needed to clarify the employment rules for personal assistants, including payment of tax, National Insurance and liability insurance.

## INDEPENDENT LIVING FUND

Some severely disabled people receive money from the Independent Living Fund (ILF) which they can use to pay for personal care to help them remain in their own homes. Recipients must qualify on both care and financial grounds.

There are two parts to this fund: the Independent Living (Extension) Fund continues payments to people who were being supported by the ILF before November 1992. A new fund – the Independent Living (1993) Fund – was set up in April 1993, and is administered by local authorities.

The old ILF was open to people aged 16 or over, whereas the new ILF is limited to people between the ages of 16 and 65 (although payments to existing recipients can continue after this age). Payments can only be made to people for whom the local authority is already providing a care package worth at least £200 per week (net of charge), up to a maximum of £500. In the early days of the reforms, few applications were made for the new fund, partly because local authorities spent such large sums on only a very few people, and partly because of strict eligibility criteria and because people did not know about it.

The exclusion of people aged over 65 from the new ILF is a major source of discrimination against severely disabled older people who wish to remain in their own homes. This discrimination is reflected in the policies of some local authorities, which have set lower maximum spending limits for care packages for elderly people than for younger people.

# Tripartite contracts

People have suggested that there should be a 'tripartite contract' – that is, a contract between the service user and the local authority; between the local authority and the provider; and between the provider and the service user. Some people supported by local authorities in charitable care homes have arrangements like this. The contract then sets out the links between all three participants in the arrangement. In some cases, the service user makes some payment directly to the service provider, with the local authority paying the balance of the cost of the service. This gives the service user direct power as a consumer and purchaser of the service.

A provision in the NHS and Community Care Act (section 42(3)) amends the 1948 National Assistance Act (Section 26(3A)) to allow for such an arrangement if all those involved agree. This was seen as necessary for schemes funded by the Housing Corporation. The Government has stated that where this happens – or, in addition, where someone else is making a contribution to the fee – the local authority continues to have ultimate liability for paying the full cost of the fees if either the resident or others involved do not pay the necessary amount (see p 159).

Even where there is not a formal tripartite arrangement, it is important that users should have full information about what they can expect from the service and what their obligations are.

# Value for money and quality

Increased competition will result in better value for money only if the effect of the competition is to keep prices down without reducing quality.

Fears have been expressed that the contracting process may force prices down at the expense of quality of care – perhaps resulting in a 'two-tier service', where people who can pay for their care get good quality care, while those needing support from public funds get a lower standard. It is important for service users that monitoring ensures that services are of good quality, regardless of who is paying.

The purchasing and contracting process should have a number of advantages over previous arrangements. These include the contract itself – a statement of what a service should provide, and how this will be monitored. Whether service users benefit from this process depends on how much choice they are offered within the contracting system, and on how well checks for quality are made. There is as yet little evidence that service users are involved in contract specifications and monitoring.

Contracting has forced local authorities to look more closely at the cost of different types of services – both provided by themselves and from independent sector providers. The Government's aim of achieving a mixed economy of care has also highlighted the nature of the relationship between local authorities and different parts of the independent sector. Voluntary organisations face real changes in their work and how it is funded; all organisations increasingly compete for contracts. The balance between centralised contracts and 'devolved budgets' will continue to evolve, with many commentators emphasising the importance of funds being managed as close to the user as possible. However, the extent to which this is possible also depends on the overall availability of resources, a subject to which we return in Chapter 8.

# 6 Complaints Procedures

In local authority social services departments, complaints procedures should be an important way of finding out how users feel about services. A complaint could be about the way a service is delivered, or the attitude of staff; about refusal of service; or about a delay in receiving a service. A complaint could also relate to failure to provide a particular service at all.

Complaints procedures are a process by which users can comment or complain, and staff and managers can respond. Complaints procedures are part of *quality assurance* – the way we keep track of how well services are doing. They help people offering services to learn from their experience, and to develop better services in the future. They offer service providers the chance to apologise and to make amends if things have gone wrong and to take steps to make sure that the problem does not arise again.

## COMPLAINTS OR PROBLEMS?

Nobody likes complaints. When you think you are doing a good job, it is not very nice if someone says they do not like the way you do it. And people often feel guilty if they complain about services or help they are receiving – it somehow seems ungrateful. They do not want to be labelled as moaners, and they certainly do not want to lose the service, or risk bad treatment as a result of their complaint.

In a way, it is a pity that the procedure is labelled 'complaints'. Some examples of when people might need a complaints procedure will show that we are often talking more about 'problems' than 'complaints'.

**Mrs Alberts** attends a day centre three times a week. The people who attend the centre have got into the habit of sitting in the same place every day, which means that Mrs Alberts ends up sitting next to Mrs Thomas, who has great difficulty speaking because she has had a stroke.

Mrs Alberts would dearly love to have someone to chat with, perhaps on one day a week. She knows how important it is for Mrs Thomas to have a chance to talk, but she finds it frustrating not to be able to exchange news and views with someone else a bit more freely.

Mrs Alberts is not exactly sure how to tackle this. She doesn't want to appear to be a grumbler, and she certainly doesn't want to hurt Mrs Thomas' feelings.

In the language of the community care reforms, Mrs Alberts should be able to express her views through the *complaints procedure*. It should be possible for her to sort out this problem through the *informal* part of the procedure, by having a quiet word with a member of staff, who should be able to respond sympathetically. If the staff member does not know how to sort it out, they should know who will be able to.

Some problems are more serious, and may need to be dealt with through the *formal* part of the complaints procedure.

**Mrs Akram** has had a home care worker three mornings a week for some time. Unfortunately, the worker has been ill, and several different workers appear to be filling in. None of them can speak Mrs Akram's own language, and she finds it difficult to understand what is happening. Her daughter has raised the matter with the home care organiser, who has said that nothing can be done. They are very short staffed, and her mother is lucky to have the service.

People like Mrs Akram and her daughter are often worried or confused about the service they are receiving, but they are not sure how to go about setting things right. They are often afraid that the service will be taken away if they complain. Sometimes it seems that anything is better than nothing. But is it? Mrs Akram's daughter may decide to take this problem a bit further – through the formal complaints procedure of the social services department. She will 'register' a formal complaint on behalf of her mother.

# HOW A COMPLAINTS PROCEDURE SHOULD WORK

## The White Paper and the Act

As already seen in Chapter 2, the White Paper (para 5.7) emphasised the importance of learning about the views of users and carers. It saw complaints procedures as one way in which this could be done (para 3.4.10). The NHS and Community Care Act confirmed this in law.

Section 50 of the 1990 Act amends section 7 of the Local Authority Social Services Act 1970. New sections inserted into the 1970 Act say that the Secretary of State for Health can by order require local authorities to

> establish a procedure for considering any representations (including any complaints) which are made to them by a qualifying individual, or anyone acting on his behalf, in relation to the discharge of, or any failure to discharge, any of their social services functions in respect of that individual.
>
> section 7B(1)

Someone is a 'qualifying individual' if '(a) the authority have a power or a duty to provide, or to secure the provision of, a service for him; and (b) his need or possible need for such a service has (by whatever means) come to the attention of the authority' (section 7B(2)).

The Complaints Procedure Directions were issued to local authorities in 1990, and printed as an appendix in the Policy Guidance, which also gives fuller details of what is expected of local authorities in setting up complaints procedures. The Department of Health also issued Practice Guidance to local authorities (*The Right to Complain*), giving more detailed information about how local authorities might approach the complex task of making complaints procedures work.

Social services departments should have information easily available which tells people how to comment on or complain about services provided or arranged by them. A user of services might wish to use the complaints procedure, or perhaps someone who has been told that nothing is available but who believes that a service should be arranged for them.

Someone else can make a complaint on behalf of such a person – perhaps a relative or friend who can see that things are not going well. Carers might also wish to make a complaint, if they do not feel that their interests are being properly considered.

# Essentials of a complaints procedure

There are certain things which must be part of every local authority's complaints procedure. These are described in the Policy Guidance, and are summarised in this chapter.

## OBJECTIVES OF COMPLAINTS PROCEDURES

The Policy Guidance sets out objectives for complaints procedures. Complaints procedures should:

*(i) provide an effective means of allowing service users or their representatives to complain about the quality or nature of social services;*

*(ii) ensure complaints are acted on;*

*(iii) aim to resolve complaints quickly and as close to the point of service delivery as is acceptable and appropriate;*

*(iv) give those denied a service an accepted means of challenging the decision made;*

*(v) provide in defined circumstances for the independent review of a complaint;*

*(vi) give managers and councillors an additional means of monitoring performance and the extent to which service objectives are being achieved.*                                                                   para 6.10

The Policy Guidance says that the starting point for complaints procedures is to protect the interests of individuals:

The spirit in which complaints procedures are implemented will largely determine their effectiveness ... they are most likely to ensure quality and protect individuals when they stem from a recognition of users' needs and rights. They will fail to be effective if they are perceived by managers or staff as a threat.                                                                   para 6.6

A report about complaints must be given each year to the social services committee. This is part of quality control. Complaints should be used as a way of checking on how services are doing, and to see where gaps may exist. Records of complaints should feed back into the planning process to see if new or different services are needed, or if additional staff training is required.

A complaints procedure should have three stages:

**the informal or problem-solving stage**

**the formal or registration stage**

**the review stage**

# The informal stage

If a person has a problem, the aim is to sort things out as quickly as possible, preferably where the problem arises. This will involve informal discussion between the user of the service and the staff. The user needs to know what the service is meant to offer, and how to make a comment or complaint if necessary. Staff and managers of the service have to be able to accept that a comment or criticism is not necessarily blaming them: it is a way of helping to make sure that the service is as good as possible.

# The formal stage

If the complainant – the person complaining – is not happy with the result of the informal process, he or she may wish to register a formal complaint. This should be done in writing, and the complainant should be offered information about how to do it, and assistance if necessary. Complainants should be told how to find an *advocate* if necessary, to help to put their point of view (see p 86 for more about advocacy).

There should be one person – the *designated person* – in the social services department with special responsibility for the complaints procedure. This person is responsible for setting time limits for dealing with complaints, and for making sure that proper records are kept about complaints. The local authority must investigate the complaint and reply within 28 days, or tell the complainant why it has not. In any case, there must be a reply within three months, although these timescales are not always met in practice.

# The review stage

If the complainant is still not satisfied with the authority's response, he or she can have the complaint put before a *review panel*, which is described in the Directions and the Policy Guidance. There must be three people on the review panel. At least one of these must be *independent* – someone who is not involved with the local authority. Such a person could be a member of a local voluntary organisation, for instance. Local authorities are encouraged to provide training for people who serve on review panels.

The review panel will investigate the complaint, perhaps interviewing the people involved, and must report in writing to the local authority and to the complainant within 28 days. Within 28 days of that, the local authority must give the complainant a decision in writing, stating the reasons for the decision and the action to be taken, if any.

The aim is to solve problems as quickly and as informally as possible. If systems are working well, few complaints should have to be made through the formal part of the procedure. Many users simply wish to be listened to and taken seriously.

---

**COMPLAINTS PROCEDURES: CHECKLIST**

In order to be effective, a complaints procedure should have certain characteristics:

- It should be acceptable to staff and users.
- It should be clear who is responsible for handling complaints.
- The procedure should be widely available and publicised.
- There should be an informal procedure – simple and quick, involving discussion and negotiation; a formal procedure – written, with a set timescale, and a report to the user; and some form of appeal or review.
- Advocates should be available to represent the interests of users who need such help. Interpreters should also be available.
- Confidentiality should be ensured.
- Complaints – both formal and informal – should be monitored and recorded.

---

## How the procedure might work in practice

Let us look again at Mrs Alberts (see p 122). If the day centre has a complaints procedure, it will have made sure that Mrs Alberts knows what services the day centre offers and how she can comment if she wishes to. She can speak to any worker at the day centre. The workers should all have had training in how to handle comments and complaints. If the worker does not feel able to deal with the problem, they should mention it to the person responsible for dealing with complaints. The organiser then has a quiet word with Mrs Alberts, and they work out together what is the best thing to do. They may perhaps talk about it generally with everyone who attends the day centre, and the staff, and arrange that one day a week people will sit together to share activities, rather than just social time. In this way, Mrs Alberts finds new companionship, but Mrs Thomas is not singled out as the cause of a problem.

A record is kept of the complaint, and the action taken. From time to time this record is checked, to make sure that the same kind of complaint is not coming up over and over again, or to see if some new kind of service or help is needed.

What about Mrs Akram (see p 122)? An informal approach to the home care organiser did not work. The authority has money problems. They are hard pushed just to arrange services for everyone who has been assessed as needing them. So Mrs Akram's daughter submits a written complaint, and goes with her mother to see the person responsible for complaints. The complaint is about how the service is being delivered, and also about the way the home care organiser responded to the initial complaint. Mrs Akram and her daughter would like an apology about this response, reassurance about how such approaches will be handled in future, and an appropriate home care service which recognises Mrs Akram's needs.

The complaints officer looks into the problem and finds that there is a local agency which provides care workers from different local ethnic minority communities. Everyone agrees how important it is for Mrs Akram to have appropriate services, and arrangements are made for the local authority to pay this agency to provide the care she needs.

The complaints officer makes a report of the complaint and how it was handled. He or she discusses it with the home care organiser, to try to sort out a better way of dealing with problems facing service users at a time of staff shortages. They decide to contact all their home care clients, explaining the problems they are facing and inviting anyone with problems to let them know. The record is fed back into the planning system. It is decided to find out just how many home care users have the same kind of problem as Mrs Akram. Perhaps next year a larger contract for home care services can be arranged with the agency.

They also prepare a leaflet describing the home care service in a number of languages, and make sure that it is widely available.

These examples show different kinds of complaints and complaints procedures. The law and the guidance say that the social services department must have a formal, written complaints procedure. Other places will need complaints procedures as well.

# What organisations should have a complaints procedure?

If users of community care services are really to be encouraged to have their say, there needs to be a complaints procedure wherever services are provided.

## Other statutory bodies

Many community care services are provided or arranged by other authorities or organisations – for instance health or housing. Where the local authority has arranged a service which is being provided under agreement by another authority as part of a 'care package', there should also be agreement about how a person can comment or complain, if necessary.

But some people are using services without having come into contact with the local authority. Such services are still part of 'community care'. Each part of the health service, for instance, has its own system for dealing with complaints. The local Community Health Council should be able to advise users about this complicated and often confusing system, which is under review. A Government-appointed committee has made recommendations for a unified complaints procedure which would be common to all parts of the NHS. To date, the Government has not acted on these recommendations.[40]

## Non-statutory organisations

We have already seen that many non-statutory organisations – voluntary groups, housing associations, residential and nursing homes, home care agencies – provide community care services. Some of these services are provided through a contract with the local authority, which is likely to require the service providers to have a complaints procedure of their own. If the user is not satisfied with this, he or she can still use the formal local authority procedure.

Even when such services are not linked by contract to the social services department, they should have a well-thought out complaints procedure. This does not mean just handing a bit of paper to users – for instance people in care homes – with a list of names saying what to do if there is a complaint. Too often we hear from people who say they do not dare to make a complaint, even though they know what they are supposed to do in theory. People must be encouraged to believe that it is all right to say how they feel, and staff need help in learning how to deal with comments and complaints. Otherwise, the whole exercise is meaningless.

## Complaints vs appeals?

As well as enabling users to say how they feel about services they are receiving, complaints procedures can also cover instances when services are *not* provided. This will probably be most important in relation to the assessment procedure which we discussed in Chapter 4.

If people who feel they need a service are not happy with the assessment, or with services offered as a result of the assessment, they must use the complaints procedure to have this reviewed. So although this chapter is mainly about service users saying how they feel about a service, it is also relevant in situations where people feel they have been denied a service unreasonably, or wish to challenge the local authority about the services it is offering to them. For instance, some people have used the complaints procedure where they have had to face a long wait for an assessment, or where there have been problems in obtaining an adaptation to their home.

This means that the complaints procedure is not only an important *problem-solving* process, but also an *appeal* process for the assessment system. Many people feel that it would be better to have a special review or appeal system for the assessment procedure, and leave the complaints system for services which are actually provided.

# WHAT HAPPENS IF THE COMPLAINTS PROCEDURE FAILS?

Complaints procedures are one way for service users to make their voices heard. But what if things are still not right? Where else can people turn?

## The Local Government Ombudsman

The Policy Guidance states that complaints procedures must include information about how to take a problem to the Local Government Ombudsman.

The Ombudsman exists to look into cases of *maladministration* in local government that cause injustice. Maladministration occurs when a local authority has not carried out its work in a proper way.

It could be that a service user does not believe that the local authority has investigated a complaint or followed appropriate procedures in carrying out an assessment. If the service user or his or her representative wishes to make a complaint of maladministration against the local authority, they can contact the office of the Ombudsman, who will look into the matter and advise as to whether this could be a case of maladministration. If they judge that it might be, then an investigation is carried out.

A complaint to the Ombudsman may result in the problem being sorted out after a relatively brief informal investigation. If more complex work is necessary, it can take well over a year to resolve: the average is now 74 weeks for all cases. Either way, it is an important check on the way local government works, a way of ensuring that the proper processes are observed in providing public services. The address of where to write to find out about the Local Government Ombudsman is listed at the end of the book (p 197).

## The courts

The courts may also be used to challenge the local authority about failure to provide a particular service. The NHS and Community Care Act lists the Acts under which community care services may – or must – be provided. These are described on page 77 and in Appendix 2. The

Chronically Sick and Disabled Persons Act is described on page 79. If people feel that they are not being offered a service which should be available under one of these Acts, they may be able to take an action through the courts.

It is possible to sue the local authority for breach of its statutory duty. This means, for instance, that it is not providing a service which it has a duty to arrange. It is also possible to seek a *judicial review*, a procedure through which the High Court supervises public bodies and makes sure that their actions are legal, rational and reasonable. A judicial review looks at the local authority's power or discretion and whether this has been exceeded or misused. The court can set aside a local authority's decision, but cannot impose a decision of its own. Decisions under judicial review form case law which can be used in other cases.

In Yorkshire, for instance, a judicial review has confirmed that a local authority must take account of an individual's preferences in deciding on care. Another case looked at the role of the review panel in the complaints procedure.[41] In Gloucestershire, at the time of writing, the local authority is being challenged for removing services from a user who continues to need them. The authority claims that it has no option because of a shortage of resources.

# Default powers

People can also seek redress through the Secretary of State for Health, who can make an order to say that an authority is 'in default' if he or she 'is satisfied that any local authority have failed, without reasonable excuse, to comply with any of their duties which are social services functions' (section 7D of the Local Authority Social Services Act 1970, as amended by the NHS and Community Care Act 1990, section 50). This is called a 'default power', and the Secretary of State can order the local authority to comply with a particular duty. Decisions by the Secretary of State under default powers are not made public.

The Public Law Project (address on p 198), itself a charity, has published a briefing called *Challenging Community Care Decisions*. It aims to help voluntary organisations and lawyers to advise people who are unhappy with community care decisions or procedures, and to identify test cases which may lead to improvements in community care practice and provision.

# ENCOURAGING PEOPLE TO MAKE COMPLAINTS

Even when everyone works hard to make sure that a service is as good as possible, there are times when problems come up which are not tackled. There are probably many reasons for this. One important barrier to an effective complaints procedure is diffidence about complaining.

When we use a service which is provided by 'experts' or 'professionals', or when we are very dependent on a service, we naturally feel nervous about expressing our feelings. (This can also happen during an assessment.) We know that the 'expert' is very busy and we do not want to waste their time. We may be afraid that complaining will mean losing the service altogether. There is often a fear of retribution. Staff who work under great pressure, or for low pay, may also worry about their jobs, and react defensively when they feel criticised.

There may be a problem with communication: some people with community care needs may not be able to express their views, either because of their illness or condition, or because they do not speak English well enough.

Many people do not know what they ought to be able to expect from a service. They may not believe that anything can or will be done to sort out the problem.

**A complaints officer:** 'Mainly we've had complaints about children's services under the Children Act. It's mainly relatives who complain about services for older people.'

Many authorities have not yet succeeded in making complaints procedures widely known and understood. People contacting the social services department to ask for help often have no idea what to do if they are not happy with the response. Sometimes there are no standards for services clearly stated, so users do not know whether they have a legitimate complaint. (This and many other related issues are discussed in an early Department of Health monitoring study: *Implementing Community Care. Informing users and carers.*)

Some authorities and service providers work very hard to take complaints procedures seriously, and to encourage users to express their views. One way of doing this is for local authorities to check on all services, to find out how easy it is for people to make comments or complaints. Staff can be trained and encouraged to look around, and take note when they observe things which might not be quite right.

Other providers may discourage comments, in the belief that 'we are doing a good job' or 'doing the best we can'. 'People come so there can't be any problems – we're full' is often used as evidence of a good service, despite the fact that no other similar service may be available.

People who do complain – or express their views – frequently find that this *does* improve things. Perhaps a member of staff really has been mistreating someone; perhaps the food really is not adequate. Complaining is difficult, but if no complaint is made then the bad practice is certain to continue. Sometimes responding to a comment or complaint will mean explaining honestly why a particular thing *cannot* be done. Trying to protect people from the truth about lack of money or resources can seem to them like being fobbed off with no information at all.

Making complaints can also be a problem for staff who see bad practice, but who fear for their jobs if they complain. Talking to someone in confidence outside the place of work may help to get the problem looked into and put right. However, 'whistle-blowing' often leads to the loss of a job. It is not easy to do. The Government has issued guidance on 'whistle-blowing' in the NHS, but concerns remain about problems for staff who do speak out.

## Advocacy and complaints

Some people will need an *advocate* (see p 86). They may not be able to express their own views, perhaps because they cannot speak after a stroke, or because they suffer from dementia. The Government's Directions to local authorities on complaints procedures state that they must offer 'assistance and guidance' to the complainant or give advice on where it can be obtained. Some local organisations may have specially trained people who can act as advocates.

The Practice Guidance on complaints procedures recommends that social services departments should consider keeping a register of agencies and individuals that might provide help and support to clients. Although advocacy has been developed in some areas, it is still relatively uncommon for older people.

## Confidentiality and complaints

People want to be sure that their complaint is treated confidentially. No one likes to have their problems talked about by others. When people are frail or vulnerable, it is particularly important that their right to dignity and privacy is respected at all times. Respecting confidentiality is one important way of doing this.

The Practice Guidance sets out principles of confidentiality:

> that information should only be used for the purpose intended;
>
> that information should normally be shared only with the consent of the individual user/carer;
>
> that information should only be shared between agencies on a 'need to know' basis. *The Right to Complain*, para 6.30

The need for confidentiality when dealing with complaints should be an important part of training for all staff and helpers.

## Overcoming the influence of ageism

Another barrier to an effective complaints procedure is the influence of 'ageism' – having negative or preconceived images about what older people will be like *just because they are old*. In general, our society attaches glamour to being young. Many people fear growing old and becoming dependent. Popular fashion and music all focus on slim, trim images of youth. Birthday cards joke about each additional year – 'over the hill' at 40, for instance. Sports broadcasters call competitors 'geriatric' when they are in their 30s. Doctors advise older people to 'learn to live' with aches and pains, often asking 'What do you expect at your age?'

It is certainly true that as we grow older, we can expect changes. Ageing is a gradual process which takes place throughout our lives, but growing older is *not* a time of inevitable dependency.

If people working in community care expect old age to be a time of decline, they will not see the full potential of the help they can offer nor will they expect older people to say how *they* feel about the services they need. They will see an 'elderly person' instead of a 'person' who has his or her own history, desires and wishes. They may offer a service they think is 'best', but which does not meet the needs of that particular person. It is interesting in this respect that the Social Services Inspectorate has found evidence that 'often the needs of older people seemed to be seen as homogeneous . . .' (*Implementing Caring for People. Community care packages for older people*, para 1.3).

Ageism also affects the expectations of service users themselves. Older people are often reluctant to 'bother' anyone about their problems. They may not be aware of what can be achieved. They may need help to believe that their situation can be improved.

Racism and sexism also impose preconceived stereotypes which intrude on people's individuality and expression of their needs. If meaningful complaints procedures are to be set up, all such attitudes will have to be challenged.

---

In this chapter we have seen that complaints procedures cover both service provision and appeals about various types of decision. There is considerable evidence of variation in local authorities' complaints procedures and of varying levels of success and satisfaction for people making complaints.[42] Some of these problems arise because of the lack of formal appeals procedures for assessment decisions and charges for services, and because of the overlap between housing and social services departments in administering disabled facilities grants.

There is much talk these days about 'charters'. Indeed, from April 1996 local authorities must have their own community care charters. The Government's *Framework for Local Community Care Charters in England* includes a section called 'If things go wrong'. This talks not just about complaints procedures but also about putting things right, and fully explaining and apologising to those involved.

A good complaints procedure is not a 'moaner's charter'. Nobody has the right to complain just for the sake of it. But it is a fundamental principle of the Citizen's Charter initiative. It should be the foundation of a 'user's charter' which encourages users of services to have their say and helps everyone involved to see services as belonging to the users and meeting their needs.

# 7 Inspection and Quality

Like 'complaints', the word 'inspection' can create negative images. It sounds like something that is 'done to' people or services – and, of course, in one sense it is. However, inspection can and should be much more than that. It should be one of the many ways in which we help improve the *quality* of all care services.

From April 1991, local authority social services departments have been required to have 'inspection units'. Local authorities are responsible for *registration* of private and voluntary residential homes, and for *inspection* of all residential homes in the area, including those run by the social services department itself. Inspection units may check on day care or home-based services arranged or provided by the local authority, but they are not required to do so. The units also have responsibilities under the Children Act 1989.

## WHAT IS AN INSPECTION UNIT?

The White Paper *Caring for People* said that local authorities should set up independent inspection units to inspect and report on both local authority and registerable independent residential homes. Local authorities already had a duty to register and inspect *independent* homes, but they did not have to inspect their own homes. This sometimes meant that local authorities set standards for private and voluntary residential homes which were not met in their own homes.

Section 48 of the NHS and Community Care Act 1990 gave new powers to local authorities to inspect their own homes. A statutory Direction

(LAC(90)13) set out local authorities' obligation to do this. This Direction has subsequently been replaced by Inspection Units Direction 1994, as part of Department of Health Circular LAC(94)16.

To ensure that they carry out such inspections fairly – or even-handedly – the inspection units have to be set up so that they are 'independent of the day to day management of local authority homes' (*Caring for People*, para 5.19). The units have to be responsible to the Director of Social Services but they are meant to be separate from direct management of homes, or other services which they may eventually inspect. This has led to the units being referred to as at 'arms-length' from the direct provision of social services.

# What do these units do?

As with everything to do with community care, the way the units are set up and their exact tasks are different in each local authority. Some authorities have brought complaints, registration and inspection, and standard-setting into a unit which might be called 'Quality Assurance', or 'Quality and Standards'.

Much of the work of inspection units with residential homes is based on requirements set out in the Registered Homes Act 1984 and Regulations related to this Act. The inspection unit's tasks include:

- registration of private and voluntary residential homes. This task does not include registration of nursing homes, which is carried out by the registration officer of the District Health Authority;

- inspection of all registered residential homes in the area with four or more residents;

- working with residential home proprietors to improve the quality of care;

- setting standards which homes are expected to meet;

- making publicly available reports to the social services committee about individual inspections, and about the work of the unit in general;

- developing a policy statement on following up inspection reports;

- working with an advisory panel and seeking the views of users of care and their relatives or representatives;

- using their work to feed back into the planning and purchasing and contracting systems.

# REGISTERING
# RESIDENTIAL HOMES

**Mr and Mrs Anderson** live in a large house with several spare rooms. The couple have always enjoyed the company of older people, and Mrs Anderson worked for many years as a state enrolled nurse. For several years, they cared for two older people, treating them as part of the family. Because they cared for fewer than four people, up until April 1993 they did not have to register as a residential home. Nor did they have to be inspected as a residential home by the local authority.

However, the Registered Homes (Amendment) Act 1991 provided that from April 1993, people who run 'small homes' must be registered under a simplified procedure. Instead of doing this, Mr and Mrs Anderson decided to devote more time and resources to helping dependent people to live a fulfilling life. They decided to build an extension to their home, and become fully registered. Mr and Mrs Anderson had to give a lot of thought to this venture. Their first step was to contact the inspection unit of the local authority, to find out what they would have to do in order to be registered to run a residential home.

One part of the inspection unit is responsible for registering homes under the provisions of the Registered Homes Act 1984.

## Registerable homes

A 'registerable home' under the Act is one that provides 'board and personal care' for people who need such care 'by reason of age, disablement, past or present dependence on alcohol or drugs or past or present mental disorder'. Residential homes are not allowed to provide 'nursing' care, although such care can be brought in for a resident, or provided under the supervision of a district nurse.

As we have already mentioned, small residential homes for three or fewer people have also been required to be registered from 1 April 1993. The discussion about residential homes in this chapter relates mainly to homes with four or more residents. Little is known about the workings of 'small' homes.

Certain homes do not have to be registered: they are 'exempt'. These include homes provided by any organisation constituted by Act of Parliament (this includes homes run by the local authority) and homes run by an organisation incorporated by Royal Charter.

# Requirements for registration

Requirements for registration of residential homes for four or more people are contained in the Registered Homes Act 1984 and in the Residential Care Homes Regulations 1984. The local authority has to be sure:

■ that the applicant for registration or any other person concerned with running the home is a 'fit person' to be involved with a residential home (this is the only registration requirement for a 'small' home);

■ that the premises are 'suitable' for the purpose of the home;

■ that the way it is intended to run the home will provide the services or facilities reasonably required.

It is important to remember that the home itself is not what is registered but the person (or persons) responsible for running the home (the owner and/or the manager).

Once a home is registered, it must display a registration certificate showing the name of the person registered; the total number of residents for whom both board and personal care are to be provided; and the age, sex and category of people who may be cared for.

The law does not define a 'fit person' or 'suitable premises'. Each local authority therefore interprets the rules in its own way. Thus neighbouring authorities may have different requirements for residential homes. For instance, many authorities have restrictions on the size of home they will allow, although there is no 'ideal' size for a home. If a proprietor believes that the authority is interpreting the Regulations unfairly, he or she can take the matter to a Registered Homes Tribunal.

Many people believe that there should be national standards or guidelines which homes in all areas should have to conform to. Some national organisations operate homes in different parts of the country. They find themselves having to work to different standards set by the various local authorities.

Concern also arises because neither the law nor the Regulations require homes to have written contracts with residents, setting out what they can expect to receive from the home in return for their obligation to pay the fees. At present, the home's obligation to provide a contract can be fulfilled by statements about the home's facilities in the brochure. A formal contract between the resident and the home is particularly important where people are not supported by the local authority. Some inspection units recommend that all homes have contracts with residents as a matter of good practice, although such contracts vary in content enormously.

## THE FACILITIES AND SERVICES RESIDENTIAL HOMES MUST PROVIDE

According to the Regulations, the person registered must run the home so as 'to make proper provision for the welfare, care and, where appropriate, treatment and supervision of all residents'.

Section 9 of the Regulations describes the facilities and services to be provided, considering the size of home and the number, age, sex and condition of residents. These include:

- employment by day and, where necessary, by night of enough suitably qualified and competent staff to be adequate for the well-being of residents;
- 'reasonable' day and night-time accommodation and space for residents;
- adequate and suitable furniture, bedding, curtains and floor coverings, and, where necessary, equipment and screens in rooms occupied or used by residents;
- the adaptations and facilities necessary for physically handicapped residents;
- adequate light, heating and ventilation in all parts of the home occupied or used by residents;
- maintenance of all parts of the home occupied or used by residents in good structural repair, clean and reasonably decorated;
- regular laundering of linen and clothing;
- arrangements where necessary for residents to receive medical and dental services;
- suitable arrangements for recording, safekeeping, handling and disposal of drugs;
- suitable arrangements for the training, occupation and recreation of residents.

There should also be facilities for visits to residents – in private if people wish. The timing and other arrangements for visiting can be decided by the person registered, in consultation with the registration authority.

Every resident should be told in writing how to make a complaint, and the person registered must make sure that any complaint is fully investigated.

# INSPECTING RESIDENTIAL HOMES

Once the registration section of the inspection unit has completed the registration process for an independent home, the law requires that homes for four or more people be inspected at least twice a year. Local authorities have to ensure an 'even-handed' approach between these inspection procedures and those which they have introduced for their own homes. They must show how recommendations made in inspection reports on homes in all sectors will be acted upon. A publicly available policy statement should be sent to everyone with responsibility for the management of homes being inspected. It should show:

- who is responsible for following up the reports to ensure that any required action on recommendations is taken;

- the time limits for follow-up action;

- how the adequacy of the response to the reports is monitored (Circular LAC (94) 16 *Inspecting Social Services*).

The Government plans to review inspection procedures in 1995, to test their independence from directly provided social services, and to make sure that the same standards are being applied to all sectors of care. In the meantime, a new requirement is introduced in 1995 for the Chief Executive of the local authority to give an annual published report to the council about:

- the unit's objectivity in applying common standards between local authority and independent provision;

- the independence of the unit within the social services department;

- the degree of open reporting of the contents of inspection reports, and their public availability;

- the effectiveness of follow-up where improvements are needed, particularly to the authority's own services (Circular LAC (94) 16 *Inspecting Social Services*).

## What is inspection?

Inspection is a process of evaluation. It considers various things which, taken together, contribute to the quality of the service. The Department of Health's 1991 Practice Guidance on inspection, *Inspecting for Quality*, says that this evaluation of a service or set of services should include:

> the resources devoted to the provision of the service;
>
> the processes involved in providing the service;
>
> the quality and quantity of service provision;
>
> the quality of life of users. para 4.1

The purposes of inspection are to help ensure that:

> the quality of life of users meets agreed standards and that individual users and staff are protected from abuse, neglect or exploitation;
>
> statutory needs are met and good practice is promoted;
>
> action is identified to improve performance against established standards;
>
> policies exist to make sure that staff recruitment and training support service development;
>
> services are cost effective. para 4.5

## What happens during an inspection?

A formal inspection usually lasts a day or longer. The inspectors make sure the registration details are correct (where appropriate), and check on the number of residents and their well-being. They look at the home itself, to see that it is in good condition, and to see whether repairs or maintenance are needed. They check on staffing numbers and training, and see that essential records are being kept properly. They try to look at all aspects of the home.

Less formal inspections are more frequent. At least one inspection a year should be unannounced. Inspectors can arrive at the home at any time, and may check more informally on how residents feel about living in the home.

In some authorities, the inspection unit does more than the minimum. One authority carries out four inspections a year. 'Our standards are high – extra money was invested in our unit *before* the cuts.'

But some authorities do not even do the minimum. In some areas, there are simply not enough inspectors to inspect all homes twice a year. In other areas, the inspection unit may focus on homes where there are known to be problems, perhaps inspecting these more often than twice a year, and seeing the 'good' homes at less frequent intervals.

The inspection unit prepares reports of individual inspections, which must be publicly available and distributed as a matter of course to the management of the service being inspected. Circular LAC(94)16 states that authorities should 'take steps to make sure as far as possible that those most directly affected by and interested in reports know of their existence and how they can obtain copies' (para 28).

Practice Guidance (*Inspecting Social Services*) issued in April 1994 suggests that to ensure openness managers should make reports available to social services staff and other staff making purchasing decisions, users and their relatives, among others. Reports should be available in libraries, CABs and other advice centres and from social services offices and care managers, as well as from the registration and inspection unit. Prospective service users, relatives and carers should be able to obtain reports easily. Reports should show how long they will be valid and when the next report is due (paras 4.10, 4.11 and 4.14).

Reports should show the difference between facts and opinions, and should make clear whether recommendations are *requirements* under the law or indications of where practice could be improved. The conclusions of the report should generally be agreed by all those involved in the inspection (paras 4.23 and 4.25).

## Lay assessors

From October 1994 certain inspections have had to include lay assessors, in line with Citizen's Charter principles. Policy and Practice Guidance issued in April 1994 (Circular LAC(94)16 and *Inspecting Social Services*) strengthened and revised the 1991 Policy Guidance in this and other respects.

The Department of Health has recommended to authorities that a lay assessor should take part in

- all full inspections of residential homes for adults which provide care for people with high levels of dependency and disability;
- all full inspections of children's homes;
- a planned full inspection of independent homes for adults not covered above at least once every three years, and annually for homes directly managed by the local authority (Circular LAC(94)16, para 14).

Lay assessors should play a full role in inspections; they should add the views of users, families and the wider community. They are defined as people

> with no direct or professional responsibility for the purchasing, provision or inspection of services who wish to contribute through inspection to the maintenance of high standards in social care, and may include present and former users, their relatives and friends.                    LAC (94) 16, para 12

Local authorities can use their discretion about how they recruit lay assessors and the terms on which they are engaged. They should take up references, make sure that assessors understand the requirements of confidentiality of information they receive in the course of their duties, and provide induction or training for assessors. Qualities which lay assessors should have include:

> observational skills
>
> communication skills
>
> the ability to distinguish fact from opinion
>
> the capacity to make judgements about the quality of services
>
> willingness to work in a team
>
> an awareness of equal opportunities issues.
>
> *Inspecting Social Services. Practice Guidance*, para 2.14

# Standards of care

It is possible for poor practice to go unchecked in homes in any sector. It may be difficult to pick up the fact that staff do not treat residents with sufficient courtesy or dignity, or that the regime of a home requires residents all to be in bed, say, by 8 pm, or that the food is inadequate.

These and similar problems do not necessarily arise through malice. By and large, the problems which arise in running homes occur for other reasons. These can include shortages of staff or funds; poor staff training; a lack of understanding on the part of the home's proprietors of the needs of residents; or frustration felt by staff because of the difficult behaviour of residents or pressure from families who may themselves be feeling guilty because they could not continue caring for their older relative.

At the same time as ensuring that statutory requirements are met, the inspection unit works with homes to improve standards of care. There are any number of ways in which this may be done. The inspection unit may advise on staff training; on equipment or alterations which would help the home provide better care; on attitudes on the part of staff or managers to residents and their relatives; on coping with difficult situations which may arise.

The unit will include in its report of an inspection recommendations for ongoing work to improve standards. Such work is endless: no care is ever 'perfect', so even a home offering very high quality care will have room for improvement somewhere. The inspection process should help to avoid complacency.

Inspection may sometimes uncover things which are totally unacceptable, such as abuse, unwarranted restraint, or too few staff for the number of residents. If the situation is bad enough, the inspection unit may serve

---

## THE IMPORTANCE OF BASIC VALUES

The inspection unit is helped in its work by a number of publications from the Social Services Inspectorate of the Department of Health. These include a workbook for inspection called *Homes are for Living In*, which stresses the importance of basic values which contribute to the quality of life of residents. These are:

**Privacy**
*The right of individuals to be left alone or undisturbed and free from intrusion . . .*

**Dignity**
*Recognition of the intrinsic value of people regardless of circumstances by respecting their uniqueness and their personal needs . . .*

**Independence**
*Opportunities to act and think without reference to another person, including willingness to incur a degree of calculated risk.*

**Choice**
*Opportunity to select independently from a range of options.*

**Rights**
*The maintenance of all entitlements associated with citizenship.*

**Fulfilment**
*The realisation of personal aspirations and abilities in all aspects of daily life.*                    *Homes are for Living In*, p 16

Where any of these ideals needs to be restricted – for instance in making decisions for people who cannot make them for themselves – the reasons for the limitations should be stated and the restrictions regularly reviewed.

notice that if changes are not carried out, they will take steps to close the home. This is of course a serious move, and one which is not taken lightly. It is extremely disruptive to residents to find that their home is to be closed and that they must move. Such a decision may be disputed by the home, which will have the right to take the decision to a Registered Homes Tribunal, which will look at both sides of the argument and decide whether the home should be closed.

As with complaints, there is a dilemma about how far to go in tackling bad practice which is not an infringement of relevant laws. One inspector believes it should be brought into the open: 'We shouldn't be taking responsibility for covering up deficiencies.' The charity Counsel and Care (address on p 197) has published a series of reports on aspects of care in homes, discussing such issues as the use of restraint, privacy, and the overall quality of life in homes.

## Physical standards

Inspection aims to promote high quality care, and inspectors look not only at standards of care in the home but also at physical standards.

There is a paradox in the inspection task. Good practice in residential homes emphasises the need for 'homely' surroundings. Yet some requirements for homes, which inspectors and others responsible must insist on, can be anything but 'homely'. Homes have to conform not only to the requirements of the inspection unit, but also to those of the Fire Safety Officer and the Environmental Health Department.

Most such requirements are laid down for the protection of people living in communal homes, where hygiene and fire safety may be of paramount importance. But for people in wheelchairs, negotiating fire doors can be difficult, if not impossible; and food safety regulations may prevent residents from participating in a 'homely' way in preparation of food. There is more work to be done on how to create a homely environment which is safe for those who live in it.

Many local authority homes are quite old, and their physical standards often fall short of those required of private and voluntary homes, although standards of care may be very good. In some areas authorities have decided to close homes or to transfer them to independent providers, rather than spend, from already overstretched budgets, the large sums of money needed to bring them up to standard. In other areas authorities are working to bring the physical standards of their own homes into line with those of independent homes.

In authorities where there are many independent sector residential homes, some authorities are focusing on improving specialist residential homes, such as for people with dementia, no longer providing any of their own 'ordinary' residential homes.

**A senior social services officer:** 'The 85 per cent rule (see pp 165–167) and the good external supply of residential care means that we cannot afford to keep our "ordinary" homes – we cannot be competitive. Apart from homes for elderly mentally ill people, we no longer provide in-house "ordinary" residential care. So much for choice and economics.'

# INSPECTING NURSING HOMES

We have seen that local authorities have powers to inspect only residential homes. Since April 1993, however, they have been purchasing places for people assessed as needing care in a nursing home.

Nursing homes are registered and inspected by the District Health Authority under separate regulations from those for residential homes. In debate during the passage of the NHS and Community Care Act, the Government was urged by many people to combine the inspection and registration system for both types of home. The argument was that it is difficult to assign people neatly into a 'nursing' or 'residential' category: older people, in particular, often have needs which fall between the two. A category of 'dual registration' does in fact exist, whereby homes are registered both as nursing homes and as residential homes. This means that if a resident develops extensive nursing needs, he or she should not have to move to another home to find suitable care. But it also means that the home has to be registered and inspected by both authorities, which can be quite a complex process.

The separate systems were not altered by the Act, so health authorities remain responsible for the inspection and registration of nursing homes with which local authorities may be placing contracts for care. This means that the two authorities have to agree on how the local authority is to have access to such homes for the purpose of monitoring how its contract specifications are being met.

Some authorities are overcoming the problem by developing joint inspection units, combining health and local authority inspection staff and developing joint working, with each continuing to be responsible for its respective statutory obligations.

## Nursing in residential homes

The blurred boundaries between 'health' and 'social' care which we discussed on pages 69–70 are evident in many residential homes, which strictly speaking should not provide nursing care. Such homes may *bring in* nursing care, but should not themselves offer it. Yet many residents in residential homes become increasingly frail and require nursing support. Such people are often very happy in the residential home, and managers who are qualified nurses may offer nursing care – against the rules, unless under the authority of a district nurse. In addition, it is sometimes said that unqualified care staff also carry out what are technically nursing duties. This may mean that residents of such homes are dependent for health care on unqualified personnel, with little protection if things go wrong.

Dual registration is one way round such problems, but it is not always appropriate, particularly for small homes for whom it may be too expensive and complicated. The increasing dependency of people in residential homes adds strength to the arguments of those who believe that the distinction between residential and nursing homes should be abolished.

# INSPECTING
# NON-RESIDENTIAL SERVICES

There is little provision for the inspection of day care services or services provided in people's own homes. There is no legislation to regulate such services, and the Government's 'Deregulation Initiative' has in recent years aimed to *reduce* the amount of regulation in general rather than to increase it.

However, there has been considerable pressure on the Government to introduce regulation for non-residential services. Under the community care reforms there are ways in which users of such services may be protected – through the assessment process, through setting standards for services and monitoring contracts, and through the complaints system. In these ways users of *contracted* services should be able to make their views known, although whether this in fact happens in practice is less certain. There is also nothing to stop local authorities allowing inspection units to include in their work day and domiciliary services provided or arranged by local authorities.

Protection through contracts does not, however, apply to people who purchase services for themselves. Service providers are concerned about the lack of regulation, and have joined together to produce their own standards for services. Some local authorities have set up voluntary local registration schemes, which might be based on these standards, which have been produced by the Joint Advisory Group of Domiciliary Care Associations.

The Department of Health Social Services Inspectorate has also published information to help people develop standards for domiciliary services. *Inspecting for Quality. Developing quality standards for home support services* is a handbook for social services managers, inspectors, users of services and their relatives and friends. However, concerns remain that there is no statutory regulation of services for people in their own homes or day care services.

**A social services officer:** 'Domiciliary care should have central regulation. People in their own homes are so vulnerable and they have no recourse in law when they are taken advantage of. If you are very immobile and you depend on an agency calling four times a day to ensure you get to the toilet or can eat, you ought to be able to count on that being done according to some regulations.'

The issue may be considered again in the Government's review of registration and inspection in 1995.

# SETTING STANDARDS

In carrying out its inspection work, the inspection unit should be working to standards which it has prepared, and which should be publicly available. In this way, home owners and managers, staff, residents and their families or representatives will all know what to expect of care in a home. The inspection process should thus be based on explicit values and measurable standards.

The inspection process is part of *quality control*, the process of testing how well a service is doing against standards or specifications which have been set for it. In setting out standards of care and then testing how well they are being met, inspection units should be checking on quality on behalf of service users. The inspection process is thus one way of protecting service users, although it should not substitute for other ways of helping users to express their views.

Setting standards is not an easy process. Ideally it will involve local experts, service users, central government, service providers and politicians as well as members of the inspection unit. Standards should be built around a framework of values which express the philosophy on which the service is based.

Important values in community care services are the belief in the fundamental dignity and worth of each user of services, and the importance of equal opportunities in providing services and letting people know about them. The activities and process of inspection, the Government's 1991 Practice Guidance says, should be anti-discriminatory and ensure that there is equal access to community care services irrespective of the race, culture, religion, gender, age or disability of the user.

## DEVELOPING BETTER RELATIONSHIPS

The Relatives Association (address on p 197) has been formed to bring together relatives of people in all types of care home, to help them develop better relationships with care home proprietors and staff, and to tackle some of the areas of bad practice which persist, despite all the attempts to protect the interests of residents.

Standards will also be based in part on work done by the Social Services Inspectorate of the Department of Health, and on new good practice being developed by the Residential Forum, which brings together a wide range of organisations and practitioners under the auspices of the National Institute for Social Work.

## Training and maintaining standards

Training is an important aspect of promoting standards in care, both for people directly providing services and for their managers. In recent years there has been a significant development in training for people at their place of work. National Vocational Qualifications (NVQs) have been developed for people who work in residential, day and domiciliary care (as well as in many other fields). Increasingly, their use is seen as part of maintaining the standards which are set for service providers. This should benefit workers and service users alike, creating increased job satisfaction and promoting better quality care.

## The role of users in setting standards

The views of users are particularly important for setting standards, as it is easy to develop standards which relate mainly to professional values or the values of providers. These may not always reflect the views of users.

However, as we have seen, many service users and their carers are not used to having their say. They often feel guilty about complaining or commenting, and are sometimes afraid that the service will be taken away if they say how they feel.

**An inspector:** 'It's a black hole in the inspection process – getting comments from residents or relatives . . . we don't get relatives or residents queuing up to see us because they don't know we're visiting . . . there's an unconscious fear about making a fuss. So we're actively looking at ways to get round that – we'll be posting signs a month in advance of inspections, inviting residents and relatives to put their point of view, either through the manager or directly to us.'

In order to contribute to the standard-setting process, users need:

■ information about what a service should be providing and the quality standards which apply to it;

■ the opportunity to take part in developing services;

■ help in believing that they can express their real views, and in raising what may be their unreasonably low expectations.

Such involvement will not happen overnight. There will be disagreements, and some things will not be possible, perhaps because there is not enough money or staff, or because some needs simply cannot be met. The main thing is that all this is discussed openly, and that users, purchasers and providers cooperate in deciding what standards to aim for.

---

### STANDARDS[43]

**A standard is a yardstick**

It is a way of judging how well a service is doing. It is a statement which should be able to stand up to measurement and be acceptable both to the people who must keep to it and to the people who will be served by it.

Standards for services can relate to many different aspects of a service. These can include: the law or regulations; values; rules and guidelines of the organisation (or of government); codes of practice for particular types of service, or professional standards.

Standards should be precise statements which can be measured and which can work in practice. Some standards should be achievable immediately; others can represent aims to be worked towards.

Standards can be measured or tested in different ways. Some will relate to the number of people providing a particular service for a certain number of users. Others will relate to the quality of life as experienced by users. Some will be *objective* (they can be measured or quantified); others will be *subjective* (they are about how people feel, or how satisfied they are). They may be about buildings or equipment or numbers of staff, or about attitudes and general approach.

Standards must be based on basic principles or values of service. They need to relate to what is put into a service to achieve the aims of that service and what is achieved – the outcome.

Age Concern England's publication *Gold Standards* brings together information about many different kinds of standard in providing care and services for older people.

# ADVISORY PANELS

In all its work, the inspection unit will have the backup of an advisory panel, which should meet at least twice a year. (The 1990 Direction called for an 'advisory committee'. In 1994 local authorities were instructed in a new Direction (LAC(94)16) to set up an 'advisory panel' instead). The advisory panel does not have powers to make decisions, but it advises and supports the inspection unit. It should bring in the views of residential home providers and users of care or their representatives, as well as health authority representatives and providers of other services (for example, domiciliary care).

Each local authority decides who should be on the advisory panel, but it must include at least as many lay people (as defined on p 144) as service providers, including officers mainly or wholly concerned with the provision of services. Guidance issued in 1994 suggests that the Chief Executive of the local authority might wish to be represented on the advisory panel, in view of his/her duty to present an annual report to the council on the inspection unit's work from 1995.

To avoid panels being too big, an authority might decide to have more than one, perhaps for different areas in the authority, or for different types of home.

The panel's terms of reference should include:

- advising on the most effective use of lay people in the inspection programme, including their recruitment and preparation;
- supporting the work lay assessors do;
- considering inspection reports;
- discussing the inspection unit's standards;
- commenting on the appropriateness and even-handedness of registration and inspection unit methods and procedures;
- making proposals to improve the effectiveness of the unit;
- considering and/or contributing to the unit's annual report;
- being consulted and informed about the Chief Executive's annual report on the unit (*Inspecting Social Services. Practice Guidance*).

Advisory panel meetings should be open to the public and should be publicised; minutes of meetings, reports and other papers should be open and made generally available (except in special circumstances, where legal advice may be needed).

---

Inspection units should help ensure that care for older people in residential homes is as good as possible. In some areas, where there is a strong tradition of inspection and resources are adequate to carry out the necessary tasks, this will certainly occur. But all the necessary work may not be carried out: the unit may face pressures from other work – for instance inspecting children's homes, and checking on childminders and nurseries, as prescribed by the Children Act 1989. Or there may be too many residential homes for the number of inspectors to cope with.

Some commentators have expressed doubts about the 'independence' of arms-length inspection units. In some areas, concern has been expressed about the quality of care being contracted for, when one aim is to keep prices low, possibly to the detriment of standards:

**A voluntary group organiser:** 'A number of the homes with contracts are ones we have had reservations about. How can the inspectors comment when the home is full of social services department clients?'

Some argue that the interests of users would be better protected by a fully independent inspectorate which could monitor residential *and* nursing homes, as well as other community care services. This proposal was not accepted by the Government in debate during the passage of the NHS and Community Care Act, although it proposes to review the situation in 1995.

The 1995 review is linked with a Government-wide 'Deregulation Initiative'. The aim of this initiative is to reduce the 'burden' of regulation on businesses. In 1994 the Government consulted widely on changes to the inspection and registration systems for residential and nursing homes. Although emphasising the need to protect vulnerable people, the Government stressed its desire to reduce unnecessary burdens imposed on businesses by regulation. Some controversy was generated over the amount of money, set by the Government each year, which local (and health) authorities can collect from homes for initial registration and then as annual registration fees. Local and health authorities claim that the increasing complexity of inspection and the need to protect vulnerable residents warrant higher fees. However, the Government has refused to raise the fees in recent years, claiming that the amounts available should be enough for health and local authorities to carry out their statutory duties.

This gives rise to concern about how the inspection system can work to raise the overall quality of care, as well as monitoring the extent to which the minimum legal requirements (however imprecisely defined) are being met. A report from the Royal College of Nursing (*An Inspector Calls*) illustrates concern, for instance, about wide variation in the inspection of nursing homes. No doubt these and other issues mentioned in this chapter will form part of the debate in the promised 1995 review.

In this chapter we have looked at the links between inspection and quality, and have referred to the Department of Health's own Practice Guidance on developing and monitoring standards of care. Questions arise about whether the attempt to reduce 'burdensome' regulations will interfere with the aim of inspection units monitoring both the legal requirements for homes *and* the quality of care in homes. This will continue to be an important issue.

# 8 Paying for Care

In this chapter we look at the different ways in which community care is paid for, and consider the crucial interface between health and social services in providing community care. First we discuss the charging arrangements for care in homes and care at home, before and after April 1993. It is necessary to understand these before looking at the transfer of public money from the Department of Social Security to social services authorities to help pay for the new arrangements. Then we look at some of the other sources of money which help to pay for community care, before reflecting on some of the difficult issues for the future.

## THE TRANSFER OF FUNDS

The community care reforms involve a major transfer of money from the Department of Social Security (DSS) to local authorities. As we saw in Chapter 2, the aim of this transfer is partly to limit the enormous growth in public spending on care in homes without adequate assessment of needs, and partly to make money available to provide more care in people's own homes. In order to understand what this transfer of money is expected to achieve, we need to look at the special Income Support system for residential and nursing home care that existed until April 1993, and at the changes which the post-1993 system has brought. This will affect how much new money is available to pay for care both in people's own homes and in care homes.

# Paying for care in homes before April 1993

Until April 1993, people needing *residential home* care could pay for it in three different ways. They could:

a   find and pay for a home themselves;

b   apply to the local authority for a place in one of their own 'Part III' homes, or a 'sponsored' place in an independent home – in both cases being assessed for their ability to pay the charges;

c   apply to the Department of Social Security (if their capital was no more than £8,000) for Income Support, which would bring their income up to certain national limits, depending on the type of care provided.

The situation was similar with *nursing home* care. People either found and paid for a place themselves; or were supported in a 'contractual place' by the health authority, which would pay the full cost of the place, as if the person were still a patient of the NHS; or turned to the Income Support system as above for help with the fees.

# Paying for care in homes after April 1993

Special arrangements apply to people who were permanently resident in homes as at 31 March 1993. They are covered by 'preserved rights' (described on pp 162–163) to the special rates of Income Support.

For new residents after 1 April 1993, local authorities have the responsibility of arranging residential and nursing home care for which people need support from public funds over and above any social security benefits which they receive. (Some continuous nursing care is the responsibility of health authorities – see pp 172–174.)

The options now look somewhat different:

a   People who can afford to can find and pay for a home themselves, as before. (They should, however, be able to have an assessment of their care needs if they wish.)

b   People who need residential home care but who cannot afford to pay for it themselves will have to approach the local authority for assessment to see whether the local authority will agree to place them in a home. They then have their income and savings assessed to see how much they have to pay themselves.

c   People who need continuing nursing care come under either the local authority or the health authority – depending to some extent on local arrangements (see p 173). If care is arranged by the health authority, no means test is required; if the local authority arranges care, the assessment process is the same as that in option **b**. The health authority must give approval to nursing home placements made by the local authority.

People paying for themselves in an independent home can, as before April 1993, claim Attendance Allowance or the care component of Disability Living Allowance. If their money subsequently runs low they may have to turn to the local authority for help, as described below. If financially supported by the local authority on a permanent basis, they will stop receiving Attendance Allowance or the care component of Disability Living Allowance after four weeks. The system is slightly different for people in homes for a temporary stay.

Under option **b**, a national charging system applies to people whom the local authority agrees to support in a care home. This charging procedure covers people in *all* homes where the local authority is arranging the place. The local authority pays the cost of the place, and then collects as much as possible of that cost from the person being supported, plus any 'third party contribution' if the person has chosen a more expensive home. As with Income Support, the capital limit for help from the local authority is £8,000. If a person has more than £8,000 in savings, they are expected to pay the full cost.

When supporting people with savings of £8,000 or less, the local authority carries out a means test to see how much the person needs to pay, and how much the local authority's share is.

The local authority will encourage people to make up their income by claiming as much social security benefit as they are entitled to. This includes a *residential allowance*, which is paid as part of Income Support to people who qualify on financial grounds, in recognition of some of the housing costs of their care. This benefit is paid at a uniform national rate (slightly more in London), but only to people in independent sector homes. The local authority therefore has a financial incentive to make arrangements with independent sector homes, as residents in their own homes are not eligible for residential allowance, and therefore require a greater subsidy from the local authority towards their fees.

The local authority then uses the national charging rules to assess how much of a resident's income must be paid towards the fees, after allowing at least a certain minimum sum for personal expenses. Most income, including state and occupational pensions, is normally taken fully into account (see p 161), although certain types of income are ignored, including the mobility component of Disability Living Allowance (which has replaced Mobility Allowance).

This system is similar to that which existed before April 1993 for people in homes run by the local authority (Part III homes), or who were supported by the local authority in independent sector homes. The system has been aligned with – but is not exactly the same as – the Income Support system.

In view of the new charging rules, all people already in Part III homes were reassessed in April 1993 under the new system, which in most cases is more generous than the previous Part III assessment. Where it is not, transitional arrangements have helped to ensure that people were not immediately disadvantaged.

## Topping up and third party contributions

Under the Income Support system, people could 'top up' their fees if the Income Support and their own income were not enough to pay a home's fees. Under the new system it is possible to pay extra if, for instance, a person wishes to live in a more expensive home than the local authority needs to pay for to meet the person's assessed needs. Such payments are generally called 'third party contributions' as they are made by someone else on behalf of the resident. Such people – or organisations – may be asked to show that they can continue the payment for as long as the resident is likely to be in the home.

In such cases, the local authority is still responsible for the fee. Either it pays the provider, and collects from the resident their assessed contribution, plus the 'third party contribution'; or (with everyone's agreement) the resident will pay their share, plus the 'third party contribution', direct to the home, with the local authority paying the difference to the provider. If the 'third party contribution' fails to be paid, the local authority has responsibility for paying the full fee; but it has no obligation to continue the arrangement in the long term.

The provision for third party contributions has led to some confusion about just what the local authority itself should be paying. In some areas local authorities have set 'maximum' or 'standard' rates which they say are the limit which they will pay. Other authorities have a 'standard' fee but state that they will exceed this in exceptional circumstances.

Many older people and their families do not understand the system. There is some evidence that people are agreeing to pay third party contributions because they believe they have to rather than to purchase some extra care for which they are willing to pay. In general, the local authority should pay enough to meet the assessed needs of the person going into a care home. Where there is disagreement either about the amount they will pay or about the assessed needs, people need to ask for a review – if necessary using the complaints procedure – preferably *before* agreement is made to enter the home.

The difficulty with all this is that there may be little time for such negotiations. The person may be ill at home, his or her carer may not be able to cope, or a hospital may wish to discharge the person quickly. It is important that people in such situations are given accurate and full information about how the system should work.

## Early problems with the new system

Early monitoring of the new system has shown a number of problems. There is evidence of wrong information being given to people, for instance about the responsibility of 'liable relatives' to pay charges. It should be noted that a husband or wife left at home cannot be forced to reveal their assets, but might agree voluntarily to make some payment towards the cost of their spouse's care. Local authorities have been reminded that although the National Assistance Act 1948 allows them to ask a spouse, as a 'liable relative', to refund some or all of the local authority's costs in arranging a residential (or nursing home) place, 'this does not mean that an authority can demand that a spouse provide details of his/her resources, and the use of a joint assessment form ... is not appropriate' (Circular LAC(94)1, para 8).

If no such voluntary agreement is reached, the local authority may decide to ask a court to decide how much, if anything, the spouse should pay.

Problems have also arisen about the way the value of the property is treated. Some husbands and wives have been told that the value of their home must be counted when their spouse needs to go into a home. However, this is not true. The value is ignored when the spouse or unmarried partner or certain other relatives continue to live in the property: those who are aged 60 or over, children under 16 whom the resident is liable to maintain, or people who are incapacitated. The local authority also has the discretion to ignore the value of the property when certain other people live in it, for instance an elderly friend or a younger carer.[44]

The system of paying for respite care has also changed in many authorities. In the past, authorities often asked for only a minimum payment for periods of respite care in local authority residential homes. Under the new system, local authorities have discretion to continue that system, and charge what appears to them to be a 'reasonable amount'. However, many have taken the opportunity to increase the charges they make for respite care in residential and nursing homes. Many now operate the full charging procedure for respite periods, although they do not have to do so for stays of up to eight weeks (Circular LAC(94)1, para 15). Where charges have greatly increased, this has come as a shock to many older people – particularly older couples – and some feel they cannot afford this essential help.

Some couples are also affected by the way occupational pensions are treated in the calculation of a resident's income. Where the person going into a home has an occupational pension on which both have previously relied, the income of the spouse remaining at home can be drastically reduced. Local authorities have discretion in such cases to increase the resident's personal expenses allowance to help maintain the spouse at home (Circular LAC(94)1, paras 6–7). Many people – and, indeed, many local authority staff – are not aware of this discretion.

This book cannot go into details about charging, but care should be taken to obtain detailed and correct information. For instance, see Age Concern England Factsheet 10 *Local authority charging procedures for residential and nursing home care*, which is regularly updated.

## 'Preserved rights' to Income Support

Some people do not come under the new arrangements. People living permanently in private and voluntary homes as at 31 March 1993 continue to be covered under the old system: they have 'preserved rights' to Income Support. This means that people who were already claiming Income Support continue to do so, and people who were in homes but paying for themselves are able to claim the special Income Support rates if their savings drop to £8,000.

We have already noted that sometimes Income Support is not enough to pay the care home's fees. Where people have to 'top up' the Income Support from their own savings, it is possible to run out of money altogether, and no further support is available from the DSS. Such people have to look to charities or relatives – if they have them – for support. But charities are increasingly pressed to find 'topping up' funds, and face financial difficulties in keeping some people on Income Support in their own care homes. Private sector proprietors also face problems in continuing to provide care at the Income Support levels in some areas of the country.

Section 43 of the NHS and Community Care Act says that local authorities should not make arrangements for people who were in homes before 1 April 1993, except for groups specifically defined by the Secretary of State. These include people in residential homes who may be evicted, for instance because a home is closing, or because they cannot pay the fees and cannot find another home which they can afford. Local authorities can help such people find a place in another residential home, but in general cannot make arrangements for elderly people with preserved rights to move from a residential home to a nursing home or to move from one nursing home to another. Only the health authority can step in in such circumstances (in which case they would pay the full fees). These rules are described in Circular LAC (93) 6.

Calls have been made for local authorities to be able to intervene to help people with preserved rights in nursing homes or in residential homes and needing nursing care. To date no action has been taken, and the problem looks set to continue.

A small but significant number of people find themselves in the unfortunate situation of having insufficient funds to pay their home's fees and, perhaps, charges for 'extras', such as incontinence supplies. There have been calls for the Government to recognise the plight of these people by varying the Income Support rates in some areas where they are clearly inadequate and, where necessary, allowing discretion in individual cases to 'top up' Income Support with public funds. For more information see Age Concern England Factsheet 11 *Preserved rights to Income Support for residential and nursing homes.*

## Paying for care in people's own homes

All this has been about paying for care in care homes. But a major aim of the community care reforms is to make more money available to improve care in people's own homes. The charging system for what are called 'non-residential social services' – day and domiciliary services – remained largely the same after April 1993 as before. Each local authority has the power to set its own charges, which must be 'reasonable'. A 1983 Act says that if a person 'satisfies' the authority providing the service that his or her means are insufficient, 'the authority shall not require him to pay more than it appears it is reasonably practical for him to pay'.[45]

Government Policy Guidance on assessment reinforces this statement by saying that local authorities should make arrangements

> so that users of services of all types pay what they can reasonably afford towards their costs. But the provision of services, whether or not the local authority is under a statutory duty to make provision, should not be related to the ability of the user or their families to meet the costs . . . the assessment of financial means should, therefore, follow the assessment of need and decisions about service provision.                                        para 3.31

This means that people who have a problem paying for services – and many authorities are increasing such charges – should ask for a review of the charge. If still not satisfied, they should use the complaints procedure to have the matter looked at again.

Local authorities are currently expected by the Government to raise 9 per cent of the cost of their non-residential social services through charges. (The Government makes the *assumption* at present in its standard spending assessment (see p 170) that this amount is raised.[46]) In trying to raise as much money as possible, authorities have to face the dilemma that charges may stop some people from applying for help; but if they do not charge, they may not be able to provide as much help as they would like.

The Government has issued some guidance and an Advice Note about how local authorities should decide how much they will charge. There are great differences between authorities' charging policies. Some authorities treat Attendance Allowance and the care component of Disability Living Allowance as part of income, while others ignore it. Some authorities make flat-rate charges, while others have banded rates according to the income of the person or the amount of care provided. Some authorities charge people who receive Income Support – indeed, the Government's Advice Note specifically states that they 'do not consider that there should be an automatic exemption from charges' for people receiving a whole range of social security benefits (para 13).[47]

There is growing pressure for more detailed guidance to local authorities about how they should treat different benefits (particularly Attendance Allowance and the care component of Disability Living Allowance), and about what account they should take of the *expenditure* which illness or disability brings, in addition to the person's income.

It is little wonder that charging for services has caused such concern. The emphasis in the reforms has been to help people remain in their own homes. Yet the Government emphasis on the need for local authorities to raise as much money as possible has combined with pressures on local authority budgets to bring greatly increased charges for non-residential social services in many areas.

The difference between the residential and non-residential charging systems can, paradoxically, create a pressure on local authorities to place people in care homes. As we have seen, the value of people's own homes is taken into account when they go into a care home (with certain exceptions) but not when they receive care in their own homes. In some instances, local authorities are finding that older people assessed as needing care in a care home are declining such an option, preferring instead to have care *at home*, however expensive. In this way they retain the value of their property, but the local authority's costs may be much higher. Getting the balance right between assessed needs, people's own wishes, and the need to balance the books may prove increasingly difficult, partly because of limited resources and partly because of anomalies between the two charging systems.

# THE NEW FUNDING ARRANGEMENTS

In this section we look at that part of local authority finance which is directly related to the community care reforms.

Something over £2,575 million was spent on residential and nursing home care in the year up to February 1993 through the Income Support system. The transfer of some of this money to local authorities has been the subject of debate – about the amount of money to be transferred each year and about how it is distributed among the local authorities.

In reading this section, it is important to remember that the majority of local government funds come from other sources – for instance through the revenue support grant and local taxes. These are discussed on pages 170–171.

## The amount of the transfer

The money given to local authorities in each of the first three years under the transfer system represents the result of calculations as to how much the DSS *would* have spent under the old system on care in homes, less the money the DSS will still have to spend on people in homes, including the new residential allowance and ordinary Income Support.

Other money is fed into the transfer calculation – to take into account the number of people in homes who are expected to die or no longer to need the special Income Support rates, and for Attendance Allowance or the care component of Disability Living Allowance not paid, as referred to on page 158.

In 1993–94, the Government transferred some £399 million to local authorities in England in respect of what would have been spent on Income Support (the 'transfer element'), plus an additional amount for 1993–94 only (£140 million) in respect of further costs related to their new responsibilities and the implementation of the final phase of the *Caring for People* reforms. These two sums, plus money for administration of the Independent Living Fund (see p 119), made up the Special Transitional Grant (STG), £565.4 million in all. It was 'ring-fenced' for spending on community care. In England 85 per cent of the 'transfer element' had to be spent on services independent of local authorities. In 1994–95 the previous year's grant was included in authorities' ordinary standard spending assessment baseline (see p 170). Thus the previous year's grant becomes included in the baseline for calculating the new year's expenditure, and it is no longer ring-fenced.

The Special Transitional Grant in England in 1994–95 was £735.9 million. This included £64.1 million to be distributed by the Independent Living Fund. The 'transfer element' of the STG was £651.8 million. Once again, the STG was 'ring-fenced' and 85 per cent of the transfer element had to be spent on independent sector community care services, including residential and nursing home care.

In 1995–96, the previous year's STG is once again added to local authorities' standard spending assessment baseline, and the new STG is £647.6 million in England. This includes £517.7 million for the 'transfer element'; £30 million to encourage the development of home care and respite services; and £99.9 million for the Independent Living Fund.

Once again, 85 per cent of the 'transfer element' in England must be spent on 'independent sector' services. The total of such spending in 1995–96 must constitute the 85 per cent for 1995–96, plus sums equal to such spending in 1994–95 and 1993–94, as well as half such spending in 1992–93. In other words, the '85 per cent rule' means that the current year's spending in the independent sector must be in addition to such spending carried on from previous years (LASSL(94)11).

The Government has once again set out conditions which local authorities must have met in order to receive their allocations of the STG in April 1995. These conditions are similar to those imposed in previous years. Local authorities and health authorities must have reviewed and, where necessary, amended their existing agreements on 'their respective health and social care responsibilities for securing and funding continuing care packages' and on 'how hospital discharge arrangements will be integrated with assessment arrangements' (LASSL(94)10, para 2).

In this circular the Government states that forthcoming guidance to health authorities on their responsibilities for long-term health care will require them to undertake during 1995–96 a full review, in cooperation with social services, of their current commitments to long-term health care. They 'should ensure that they are securing adequate levels of provision with an expectation that some health authorities may need to reinvest in this area' (LASSL(94)10, para 4).

With respect to hospital discharge, authorities are reminded of the 'importance of avoiding inappropriate discharge arrangements for people with long term care needs' (para 6). Hospital discharge agreements should make sure that 'appropriate (inter agency) arrangements are in place in the community before the patient is discharged . . .' Authorities should agree on how they are going to audit a representative sample of discharges (para 5).

There will be another STG in 1996–97. The Government has announced that there will be additional resources of £418 million available for community care in that year, in addition to the STG monies for the previous three years, which by then will all be included within the personal social services standard spending assessment baseline. The proportion of the £418 million to be designated as STG – and therefore ring-fenced for community care – has yet to be decided.

# Distribution of the transferred money

Each year the Government and the local authority associations have had long and complicated discussions both about the amount of new money and about a formula for distributing it which meets the needs of those involved.

The transferred money has replaced money which was spent through Income Support on residential and nursing home care. But homes are spread very unevenly around the country. In some coastal areas, for instance, there are hundreds of homes, whereas in inner cities there may be only a few – sometimes none at all. Discussion has focused on whether the money should go to where the care is, or to the local authorities from which people have moved, to help them to build up services for people at home and in homes in their particular area.

In the first year of the transfer, 1993–94, the DSS transfer (£399 million) was distributed as follows: half the money was allocated according to the actual pattern of current Income Support spending for independent sector residential and nursing homes; and half was based on the standard spending assessment formula. The £140 million additional sum, paid in

1993–94 only, was all distributed according to the standard spending assessment formula.

In 1994–95 the distribution method was changed. The transfer element of the STG (£651.8 million) was distributed entirely according to the standard spending assessment formula, overriding the Government's earlier plans to phase in such distribution more gradually. This meant that some authorities received considerably less than would have been the case under the system which took account of the number of residential and nursing homes in their area, and therefore of the amount of Income Support which had previously been paid.

# Was enough money transferred?

One of the main concerns about the reformed system has been whether there would be enough new money for local authorities to carry out their new tasks – both to improve services for people living in their own homes and to support people in care homes. There have been a number of causes for anxiety. In the first year, as we have noted, the distribution of half of the STG according to previous Income Support expenditure favoured authorities with a high concentration of homes. The rapid shift to a fully SSA-based distribution has caused difficulties for those authorities which were relatively well off in the first year, while benefiting others. Some authorities do have enough resources at present, but others – led by the Isle of Wight and Gloucestershire – have declared themselves in considerable difficulties.

Additional anxiety has been caused by the move to redesignate some 'health' care as 'social' care. In particular, local authorities have been concerned that the reduced availability of NHS long-term care is placing an additional burden on local authorities, which are responsible for arranging increasing amounts of nursing home care (see pp 172–174).

It is difficult to establish whether the transferred money is, in fact, enough for the new local authority responsibilities. One problem is that no one really knows just how much is 'enough'. This figure will be affected not only by the quantity of care but also by its quality. Without standards by which to judge the quality of care, it is difficult to analyse whether authorities are spending enough on the care they provide.

Each local authority is concerned that the amount of money transferred to it for its new duties should be enough for it to do the job properly – many authorities are worried by the amount of unmet need in their areas.

The local authority associations such as the Association of Metropolitan Authorities and the Association of County Councils (which may merge in the future) continue to discuss all these issues with the Government in order to make the new system work as well as possible.

For the first four years at least, information will be published about how much money has gone to each authority from the transferred funds. Keeping track of what happens to the money is an important way of checking on how the changes are working. There is general concern about funding for community care social services after the STG is phased out altogether and the money ceases to be ring-fenced for community care (see, for instance, the Audit Commission's 1993 report *Taking Care*).

# OTHER MONEY FOR COMMUNITY CARE

The focus of the community care reforms has been on the transfer of funds. However, these transferred funds by no means represent all the money which is spent on community care.

## Other local authority spending

Local authorities have always spent considerable amounts on community care services. These include services such as home care and day care, as well as services such as retirement housing, provided by local housing authorities. Local authority funds are raised in a variety of ways (see box on local authority finance on pp 170–171).

## Community health care

Funds for hospital and community health care come from the purchasing budgets of health authorities and fundholding GPs. They cannot impose charges on individuals for NHS hospital and community health services (although dentists are able to make charges for their services). The availability of local hospital and community health care is thus outside the control of the local authority, yet is crucial to the authority's ability to arrange community care.

As mentioned elsewhere in this book, there has been general concern about the role of community health services in the overall community care picture. As people are helped to remain in their own homes, there will be increasing need for community health services. Yet it appears that the links between health and social services, and the ability to monitor what is happening, are not yet developed well enough. An early monitoring report of the Social Services Inspectorate showed that health authorities had not yet developed systems to enable them to assess and predict demand. This information is important for determining the amount of resources needed for community health services as community care demands increase, yet the SSI stated: 'Weak monitoring systems are also compounding [health authorities'] difficulties in identifying the

## WHERE LOCAL AUTHORITY MONEY COMES FROM

### The revenue support grant and standard spending assessment

The largest part of a local authority's grant from central government comes through the revenue support grant: money raised from national taxation which is given to local authorities to run the services which they are by law required or enabled to provide.

The Government decides how much it thinks each local authority ought to have to spend to provide a standard level of services – this is called the 'standard spending assessment'. Such figures as the proportion of older people in the population are taken into account when calculating the standard spending assessment for an authority.

### Specific grants

The NHS and Community Care Act created 'specific grants' – money which can be spent only on new services for certain client groups or particular tasks. To use this money, local authorities must use some of their own funds. The grants available for each authority will support up to 70 per cent of total spending, at present for the following purposes: mental illness, AIDS/HIV, alcohol and drugs, training and (for children) guardians ad litem and reporting officers. Spending of these grants does not count as meeting part of local authorities' obligation to spend '85 per cent' of the transfer element of the STG in the independent sector.

In 1995–96, the mental illness specific grant has been substantially increased to help provide new services for people with severe mental illness.

direct consequences of the community care changes from more general pressures on community health services within the NHS.'[48]

The Department of Health plans to issue guidance on 'joint commissioning' to help all services involved in community care to use their resources to work more closely with each other. At present, it is difficult to use for continued projects both money from social services and money from health authorities, except through a special process called joint finance, which has had limited success over the years.

# Housing and housing services

Housing for rent is provided mainly by local authorities and housing associations. Both are funded partly by the State. Money for housing associations is allocated by the Housing Corporation, which was set up by Parliament to fund and monitor the work of housing associations.

The grants have also helped innovative new projects to be set up. They illustrate the use of 'ring-fenced' money.

### Local taxation
Each local authority raises some funds through local taxation, formerly through rates, then through the Community Charge (Poll Tax), and since April 1993 through the Council Tax. In recent years the Government has put limits on the amounts which local authorities can raise in this way – this is called 'capping'.

### Fees for services
Local authorities also raise money through fees which they can charge for certain services. For instance, they can charge for meals on wheels, home care or home help, and day care; but they cannot charge for social work services. Assessing people for their ability to pay for social services is an important part of how community care works in any area, as we discussed on pages 163–164.

### Capital expenditure
If a local authority wishes to build new premises, or to undertake major renovations of buildings, it must apply to central government for permission to spend such money, up to certain limits set by the Government. One reason for transferring local authority services – such as care homes – to the independent sector is that capital can then be raised more freely.

Housing associations must also raise money from private financial institutions in order to build new properties.

Local authorities are actively discouraged from building new housing, with most of their finances going towards the maintenance and repair of their existing stock. They can also give grants to private owners (and in some cases to private tenants) whose homes are in need of repair, improvement or adaptation; some of this money is refunded by the Government.

The Government has cut expenditure on housing in recent years, for instance reducing the money available for disabled facilities grants.

## Individual resources

Much of the money to pay for community care comes directly from the people who need such care and their carers and families. These funds include their own income and savings and social security benefits.

Some personal spending on community care represents 'hidden' costs. These include the sums of money which people do not earn because they have taken on caring tasks which mean that they have had to stop work, or work shorter hours. People who need care also spend money on the extra costs which disability or illness can bring – for heating, transport, special food, equipment and other such items – some of which are compensated for by social security benefits.

# WHOSE RESPONSIBILITY?

We have already seen that although local authorities have the lead responsibility for community care they do not have the sole responsibility. For some people the greater part of their community care is provided outside social services – perhaps by the housing authority or a housing association, or by the health service. As already noted, there is potential for disputes to arise here.

*Caring for People* gives new responsibilities to local authorities to assess people for publicly supported places in residential and nursing homes. Yet it also states that health authorities retain responsibilities:

There will . . . always be some people who cannot be supported in their own homes. Where such people require continuous care for reasons of ill-health, it will remain the responsibility of health authorities to provide for this . . . health authorities will need to ensure that their plans allow for the provision of continuous residential health care for those highly dependent people who need it.                                                                    paras 4.20–4.21

Government guidance in early 1995 (Joint Circular HSG(95)8/LAC(95)5 *NHS Responsibilities for Meeting Continuing Health Care Needs*) confirms the statement made in the White Paper that 'The NHS is responsible for arranging and funding a range of services to meet the needs of people who require continuing physical or mental health care' (para 10). Such services include, among other things, respite health care, rehabilitation and recovery (sometimes referred to as convalescent care), community health services to people at home and in residential homes, specialist medical, nursing or other community health services in any setting (this would include specialist equipment and palliative care; it also covers nursing homes) and 'continuing inpatient care under specialist supervision in hospital or in a nursing home'.

The guidance requires health authorities to decide eligibility criteria and the pattern and level of services to meet continuing health care needs in their area. Health authorities must prepare draft eligibility criteria and levels of service by September 1995 for their purchasing year 1996–97. They must 'consult and involve fully' local authorities, all GPs, NHS and independent providers, and representatives of users and carers. Health authorities are expected to secure the agreement of GP fundholders to the relevant aspects of local criteria for continuing care: GP fundholders are expected to take these criteria into account when deciding which services they will purchase. A full list of the services which GP fundholders can purchase from April 1996 will be published in April 1995. Final details must be published in April 1996 and included in the new local community care charters to be published then. The Government has not set any national standards by which local provision can be judged. In the meantime, until the policies and criteria have been finalised, health authorities or GP fundholders should not further reduce or alter continuing health care services or hospital discharge criteria unless this has already been agreed with local authorities.

The guidance states that NHS continuing care in a hospital or nursing home should be for people where 'the complexity, nature or intensity of the patient's medical, nursing or other clinical care or the need for frequent, not easily predictable interventions, means he or she will require specialist clinical supervision from the NHS on an ongoing and regular basis' (Annex A, para E). This definition does not make clear how judgements will be made between continuing nursing care which is funded by the NHS and that which is not, although it is suggested in the same paragraph that ongoing and regular supervision would be at least weekly in the majority of cases. The NHS would also have responsibilities for those whose rapidly degenerating or unstable condition means that they will require specialist medical or nursing supervision (Annex A, para E). Those patients whose acute treatment has finished, and who are likely to die in the very near future, can choose to remain in NHS-funded accommodation where practicable.

The 1995 guidance overrides 1989 guidance on hospital discharge, and good practice is now set out in the *Hospital Discharge Workbook*. Unfortunately, the workbook makes no mention of the fact that neither health nor local authorities have the power to place people in care homes against their wishes, where they will have to pay. Much 'good practice' in hospital discharge to homes is based on the assumption that when being in hospital is deemed no longer appropriate for a person's care, but ongoing nursing care is needed, responsibility is automatically transferred to social services. For the patient this means the difference between free continuing care (which can be arranged by the health authority in a nursing home and fully funded by them) and means-tested care arranged by the local authority. The 1995 guidance states that people have a right to refuse discharge from NHS care to a residential or nursing home, but the consequences of such a refusal are not clear. Where such people have been judged by a consultant or multidisciplinary team not to need ongoing NHS care, the guidance states that other options should be explored. Where these are also refused, the guidance states that consideration will have to be given to discharge home or to some other place 'with a package of health and social care within the options and resources available'. The guidance does not show how this will be done if such care is inappropriate for the patient's needs.

A right of appeal about NHS continuing care is set out in the guidance. A patient may request the health authority where they ordinarily live to review the discharge decision. Normally the health authority will consult an independent panel, which has the 'key task' of ensuring that local eligibility criteria have been properly applied. Details of such panels have yet to be worked out. Health authorities must have arrangements to handle requests to review decisions 'as soon as practicable and no later than 1 April 1996' (para 9e).

Of course many people are happy to move to a nursing home and fund their own care, or to be supported there by the local authority. The point, however, is that many people face such major decisions without full information about the options. The new guidance states that patients must be given information either in writing or 'in other formats appropriate to their needs' (para 25) about hospital discharge. This includes written details of the likely cost to the patient of any options being discussed. It will be important that such information includes details of all the services the NHS has the power to provide and that it clearly sets out the patient's rights at the time of discharge.

## Bottom-line responsibilities

Under 'preserved rights' (see pp 162–163), some people in homes can completely run out of money, as we have seen. The question arises as to whether there is a 'bottom line' below which a person cannot fall where one authority or another accepts responsibility for care.

From April 1993, it was estimated that some 350,000 people were covered under 'preserved rights' to Income Support. As we have seen, they may continue to face problems with a shortfall in fees.

Under the new system, the local authority pays the full cost of a place which it arranges, and will assess residents for their ability to pay. There should be no question of a shortfall in fees for those who succeed in being supported, unless they *choose* to pay extra.

However, a question mark remains about whether the money given to local authorities is adequate to fund the necessary amount of continuing care; and about how health and local authorities will sort out responsibilities if demand for services is greater than either feels it can afford.

The 'bottom line' applies not only to people in care homes, but also to people in their own homes who need care and do not have sufficient resources to buy it. They will depend on the local authority to arrange appropriate social services under powers and duties set out in the laws described in Appendix 2; and on the health authority or a fundholding GP for appropriate hospital and community health services under provisions of the NHS Act 1977. The new system does not confer any new 'rights' – or entitlement to care – over and above those given by the CSDP Act 1970 (see p 79). Both local and health authorities have duties, under the National Assistance Act 1948 and the NHS Act 1977, to provide care, but these duties are not quantified. In the White Paper and elsewhere, the Government has stated that health and local authorities must work within the limits of 'available resources'.

We saw in Chapter 6 (pp 130–131) that where there is a problem, it will ultimately be up to the courts to decide to what extent statutory obligations must be met in respect of any particular person. At the moment, the new system does not help to sort out just where the 'bottom line' is.

---

This chapter has shown just some of the complexity of local authority funding for community care. As the reformed system has developed, the level of resources and the inter-related responsibilities of health and social services have become the two major subjects for consideration in analysis of the reforms. The other subjects which this book has looked at – for instance assessment and care management, purchasing and contracting, and community care planning – all both depend upon and influence overall resources and the divide between health and social care. This chapter has aimed to help readers develop an understanding of these complicated relationships.

# 9 Remembering the Person

In writing about the community care reforms and attempting to understand their complexities, it is easy to forget what should be their central focus: the person needing support and his or her carer. Reflecting on the new provisions and procedures described in this book, we could well refer back to Annie, whose last years we briefly described in the Introduction.

We could think about whether an improved assessment system would have identified Annie's needs and led to more appropriate services being arranged for her. Perhaps the workers who had contact with her could have worked in a more unified way. They could have asked her how she felt about the various services which were offered – why she rejected the meals service, how she felt about not having a home help, what she felt about her need for the security which the community alarm system might have offered. They might have tried to set up a service for Annie tailored to her specific needs, perhaps purchased from neighbours or local care agencies, rather than based solely within the existing statutory services.

On the other hand, she might have been assessed as not having high enough priority for the local authority to arrange services for her at all. Services would not have been 'targeted' on her. Her crucial need for support in order to prevent her going into a care home might then have been missed, and she might have ended up moving into a home in very similar circumstances. Thus the reforms might have made little difference to the way her story progressed.

Another way of thinking about Annie's experience of community care is to reflect on her needs and feelings as a *person*, rather than on the services which might or might not have been arranged for her. How might the ideals and the practice of the community care reforms have affected the way her care was handled?

The Department of Health has described a set of 'core values' for community care:

> a commitment to make sure that users and carers enjoy **rights of citizenship,** with equal access to service provision regardless of race, gender or disability; — not enough £ to fund?
>
> respect for people's **independence** and their right to take risks;
>
> regard for people's **privacy**;
>
> understanding people's needs for **dignity** and **individuality**;
>
> **individual choice** of services and how they are offered, within available resources;
>
> service provision in a way which helps people **achieve their own goals** in everyday life.
>
> *Care Management and Assessment. Summary of Practice Guidance,* para 81

This statement of core values is very similar to the basic values relating to residential homes which we discussed in Chapter 7 (p 145). It forms a framework for reflecting on how the practice of the community care reforms might relate to the ideals it describes.

# The rights of citizenship

Annie was fortunate in that she could take part in decisions about her care; there was no obvious discrimination in her treatment. And yet she was very limited in her ability to participate. For her last year at home she was virtually housebound, dependent on others for transport to essential health services and unable to walk out of doors. Her communication with the people offering services depended on their timetable, and on their willingness or ability to stop and talk.

The Government's core values state that there should be equal access to service provision regardless of disability, but this cannot happen if the disabled person is unable to participate meaningfully in making decisions about his or her care. Nor should the fact that people are old and disabled prevent constructive approaches to their problems.

The response to Mrs Akram's problems with the home care service (p 122) initially reflected aspects of racism. Her ability to participate in the system and in her own care was strictly limited, because she could not communicate with the people providing her care. Developing an understanding of the needs of people in such situations may not always result in the solution of their problem, but it will recognise their rights as citizens to be understood and to have access to services on the basis of their need, not limited by the chance of their race, culture, sex or disability.

## Respect for independence and the right to take risks

Independence is a difficult concept. Some people would argue that no one is truly independent: everyone depends on many other people. But in talking about community care we often talk about 'dependency', perhaps assuming that because a person needs help with, say, dressing, they are automatically dependent in other ways as well.

An important message of the reforms is that care should be about helping people with the care needs which they have, but not robbing them at the same time of their ability to take decisions about themselves, or to continue to do the things which they are able to do. This is where an emphasis on services can sometimes unwittingly undermine independence. One example is the provision of meals on wheels for someone who cannot get out to the shops. Providing transport to shops would preserve the person's freedom to choose what food to buy, even if they are dependent on someone to help them get there. Such an approach could have helped Annie to take a much more active part in her daily life.

Another aspect of independence is the difficult area of how much risk people should be allowed to take. In Chapter 4 (p 95) we saw that Mr O'Malley decided he would take the risk of remaining in his own home, rather than moving to a care home. Annie decided that she could not face the risk of falling again. Both were able to make their own decisions.

People whose decision-making capacity is adversely affected by illness or accident have decisions about their welfare made by others, to varying degrees. This can generate conflict between relatives, professionals and service users who have different views and it raises almost unanswerable questions about the basis for such decisions. At what point does a person's desire to remain in their own home become a matter of public concern? At what stage do professionals or families have the right to interfere with a person's independence?

As we saw in Chapter 4, these questions are closely linked with the development of assessment and care management systems. We have no legal basis for making decisions about care which override a person's autonomy. Government guidance emphasises the need to give support to people who cannot make their own decisions. Advocacy is particularly important in this respect. However, the speed with which decisions sometimes have to be made; the agonies which face relatives, friends and carers as they watch a loved person's mental faculties decline; and the fear that something will happen for which others will be blamed, all contribute to the difficult reality that decisions are often taken in the belief that they are 'for the good' of the person concerned. There are certainly no easy answers here, but there is much room for reflection and further thought about how society copes with these complex issues.

# Respect for privacy

Such questions are closely linked with notions of privacy. Support services have a way of intruding on privacy unless great care is taken. A contradiction arises between the belief in the importance of sharing information – between different professionals and workers, in the interests of cooperative working – and the need for confidentiality to protect the privacy of the service user.

In stressing the importance of confidentiality both in assessment and care management and in complaints procedures, the community care reforms promote the idea of privacy. Yet there may be some contradictions. Where people have complex needs, information about their 'case' may be circulated much more widely than they realise.

Another way of looking at privacy is to think about people's ability to live privately – both in their own homes and in communal or group homes. It is often difficult for people with care needs to preserve their privacy if, for instance, care workers turn up at any time, with no prior warning. Carers and the person they care for may never be able to be alone; people in homes may have to share a room. Inspection units may increasingly check on how residents' privacy is being respected, yet the very idea of 'inspection' appears to contradict the idea of creating 'homelike' places for people to live.

Once again, great care is needed to make sure that systems devised for protecting people do their job well, yet do not intrude on the privacy of the people involved.

## Respect for dignity and individuality

Respect for dignity and individuality arises from respect for the *person*. Some care needs – such as those arising from incontinence – threaten loss of dignity unless they are handled with sympathy and respect for the individual. Perhaps it is here that the *attitudes* of the service providers become paramount. If the idea is that positive steps need to be taken to minimise or eliminate the cause of the problem, then personal needs will be dealt with in a way which preserves the dignity of the person concerned. If, on the other hand, the idea is to 'get the job done', this will almost certainly be at the expense of the dignity of the person concerned.

A sense of loss of dignity may have been why Annie rejected meals on wheels. She felt demoralised as a person when the speed of delivery allowed no time for personal contact. Here, as with all the other aspects of community care, training plays a crucial role. It can help workers to develop positive attitudes towards others, respecting everyone's sense of worth; and it can teach them to carry out difficult or routine care tasks in ways which enhance rather than diminish the dignity of the person using the service.

In several parts of this book we have referred to the importance of training – both to implement the changes themselves and to improve the quality of care. The new National Vocational Qualifications (NVQs) have a major role to play in the working environment in helping care workers of all types to develop their capabilities. Training also has a role to play in bringing together people from different organisations and professions to share common themes of caring. It should also help discourage discriminatory attitudes.

Contracts are also important in ensuring that dignity and individuality are respected. The White Paper and the guidance stress the need to achieve value for money and cost-effectiveness. It is important that such aims should include the need to obtain good quality services through respect for the dignity of the service user. Service specifications should make this clear in ways which can be checked on.

# Individual choice of services and how they are offered

The idea of choice is central to the reforms, yet we have seen that some of the new procedures may actually have the effect of limiting choice. Within the framework of the reforms themselves, there may be more choice for some, and less or none at all for others. We have seen that the Government has placed a duty on local authorities to offer choice to people for whom they agree to arrange a place in residential and nursing homes.

The Government's 'core values' place 'choice' within the framework of 'available resources'. This raises the inevitable question of what are enough 'available resources' to allow what we think should be sufficient 'choice'. This issue will undoubtedly continue to be – as it has always been – the subject of much debate.

There are ways of offering choice, however, which do not require more resources to provide more or better services. They take us back to dignity, individuality and respect. They involve finding out how someone wishes to be addressed; offering genuine choice about when people eat meals or get out of bed; giving users a choice about who should be involved in providing their care. Too often all these choices are in the province of the *providers* rather than the *users*.

All the community care reforms should be ways of offering more choice to service users. Complaints procedures and inspection processes should actively aim to find out users' views, and to act on them; assessment and contracting should be carried out in line with users' views. How far these ideals are possible in reality depends partly on resources, but also on the attitudes of everyone involved. They crucially involve providers and workers learning how to work *with* rather than *for* users, in a genuine partnership of care.

# Achieving their own goals

In order to achieve their own goals, people have to know what is possible. They need to know what their rights are; what might be achieved, given their particular condition or illness; what help *could* be available; and where to turn for advice or support. This involves providing information to people when they need it, and which they can understand and use.

It also involves service providers opening out to become 'enablers' rather than narrow providers of particular services or skills. The reforms encourage multidisciplinary working – a difficult goal. But even good collaboration is not a goal in itself. It will be successful only if it succeeds in enabling service users to set their own goals and work towards achieving them.

This does not always mean more services. It may simply mean putting people in touch with information *about* their condition or problem, or creating groups of people to help themselves achieve their goals. Professional pride can sometimes cause suspicion of groups of people who may know more about coping with their particular problem than the professional. But if users are to achieve their own goals, they need to feel in control.

*Listening* – and recognising that we are all potential service users – is often the first step for providers in moving towards the goals of users. Some users may be very ambivalent about their goals, and need help in coming to terms with their changing needs. Annie could not reconcile her desire for independence with her growing fear of falling. Other users may not be able to express their own goals, and decisions may have to be taken on the basis of a judgement about what these might have been.

---

In Chapter 1, we compared community care to a jigsaw. Just some of the pieces of the puzzle have been described in this book. The community care reforms aim to improve the fit of some of the pieces, but do not cover the whole puzzle. Even the pieces themselves have different characteristics: some are organisational, professional and financial; others are about attitudes, respect and abandoning stereotypes.

Bringing the puzzle together into one unified picture is probably an impossible goal, and may not be an appropriate aim. For each person, however, it is important to work as hard as possible to ensure that their community care jigsaw fits together as well as it possibly can. This means continuing to strive to make the practice of community care for each person match as closely as possible the ideals – an ongoing and never-ending challenge.

# Glossary

This glossary explains some of the words and expressions most commonly used in talking about the community care reforms. It is not a comprehensive list; many more words are explained in the text.

**Assessment** Part of the process of care management through which a person's needs are defined and a decision is made about what help can be arranged.

**Care home** Used in this book when referring to residential and nursing homes. Where discussing one or the other, this is made clear.

**Care management** The process – carried out in various ways – of coordinating and arranging services for an individual person.

**Care manager** A person who carries out the major tasks of care management, such as assessment, preparing a care plan, coordinating services, and monitoring and review. The care manager may control a budget, but is not generally involved in providing a particular service.

**Carer** A person who provides care and support for someone, but who is not employed to do so and is not part of the 'formal' sector (local and health authorities, voluntary organisations and the private sector).

***Caring for People*** The 1989 Government White Paper setting out what it proposed to do to change the funding and organisation of local authority social services for community care.

**Community** Wherever people live is part of the community, and is their home.

**Community care** Services and support to help anyone with care needs to live as independently as possible in their home, wherever that is.

**Community care reforms** The reforms introduced by the White Paper *Caring for People*, and (in England and Wales) by Part III of the NHS and Community Care Act 1990. (Part IV governs changes in Scotland.)

**Community care plans** Required annually of each local and health authority; to include information about the needs of the local population, and priorities and targets for meeting these, and to show how local authorities plan to stimulate the 'market' for care.

**Complaints procedure** The process which every social services department must have for listening and responding to comments and complaints from users (or potential users) of services.

**Contracting** The process through which local authorities purchase services from private or voluntary organisations.

**Day care** Different kinds of communal care almost always provided away from people's homes. Most commonly run by the local authority or voluntary organisations, with paid and/or unpaid workers.

**Disabled facilities grant** Grant to help fund adaptations to the homes of people who qualify on need and financial grounds. Administered by housing departments, using central funds. Some grants are mandatory, but authorities often run out of centrally provided funds.

**Domiciliary care** Services provided in people's own homes; includes home care, sitting services and bathing services. Most often provided by the local authority, but increasingly by private and voluntary organisations.

**Griffiths Report** *Community Care: Agenda for action*, by Sir Roy Griffiths, was published in 1988 and paved the way for the community care reforms.

**Group home** A house in which people have their own rooms but there are communal facilities; staff may live in to offer support.

**Independent sector** Private, voluntary, charitable and not-for-profit organisations. For the purposes of spending the Special Transitional Grant, NHS trusts can be considered 'independent' of local authorities.

**Inspection** The process through which local authorities check on standards of care in residential homes and health authorities check on nursing homes.

**Institutionalisation** The negative effects institutions of all types have on residents and staff.

**Learning disability** Once described as 'mental handicap', or 'mental subnormality'. A permanent disability, usually occurring from birth, which affects learning abilities.

**Nursing home** Defined in the Registered Homes Act 1984 as 'any premises used, or intended to be used, for the reception of, and the provision of nursing for, persons suffering from any sickness, injury or infirmity'.

**Policy Guidance** As generally referred to in this book: *Caring for People in the Next Decade and Beyond.* Sets out what local authorities need to do to carry out the community care reforms as defined in *Caring for People* and the NHS and Community Care Act 1990.

**Practice Guidance** Gives greater detail about how local authorities might implement different parts of the reforms. See Recommended reading on pp 200–203.

**Purchaser–provider split** The term used to describe the separation of two parts of one authority: one part assesses the needs of the local population and of individuals (the purchaser) and buys services from another part of the organisation (the provider). Also used to describe divisions of responsibility in the National Health Service.

**Residential home** A place providing board and personal care for people who need it because of 'old age, disablement, past or present dependence on alcohol or drugs or past or present mental disorder'. Homes for four or more people must be fully registered and inspected by the local authority; homes with one to three residents must be registered under a limited procedure.

**Respite care** Provides a break for a carer, either on a regular basis or occasionally. May be just a few hours or for one or more weeks. May be provided in a person's own home or in a residential or nursing home or hospital.

**Ring-fencing** Reserving money to be spent for a particular purpose.

**Sheltered housing** Specially designed housing with varying levels of support, available to rent from district councils or housing associations, or to buy privately.

**Statutory sector** Organisations created through Acts of Parliament – health authorities, local authorities, central government departments.

**Targeting** Identifying those in greatest need of services, and setting priorities to meet their needs.

**Wagner Report** A 1988 report of a committee led by Lady Wagner. *Residential Care: A positive choice* set out ways of improving care in homes.

***Working for Patients*** The 1989 Government White Paper describing proposed changes in the organisation and management of the National Health Service.

# References

[1] *Community Care: The way forward* (1993) House of Commons Health Select Committee 6th Report, Session 1992–93, HC 482–1, HMSO, London; *Towards Community Care: ADSS review of the first year* (1994) Association of Directors of Social Services.

[2] *The Prevalence of Disability among Adults* (1988) Jean Martin, Howard Meltzer and David Elliott (OPCS Surveys of Disability in Great Britain, Report 1), HMSO, London.

[3] *Housing: The foundation of community care* (1989) Alison Wertheimer, NFHA/MIND, London, 2nd edition.

[4] *The Health of the UK's Elderly People* (1994) Medical Research Council, London.

[5] OPCS Monitor SS 92/2 *General Household Survey: Carers in 1990* (1992) Government Statistical Service.

[6] *Different Types of Care, Different Types of Carer* (1994) G Parker and D Lawton, HMSO, London.

[7] *General Household Survey* (1992) table 2.11, and *An Ageing Population* (1991) Fact Sheet 2, Family Policy Studies Centre, London.

[8] Virginia Bottomley, *Hansard*, 12 December 1994, col 632.

[9] Virginia Bottomley, *Hansard*, 12 December 1994, col 638.

[10] Virginia Bottomley, *Hansard*, 12 December 1994, col. 638.

[11] *Developing NHS Purchasing and GP Fundholding:* EL(94)79; *Developing NHS Purchasing and GP Fundholding: Towards a primary care-led NHS* (1994) NHS Executive.

[12] *Health Service Journal,* 20 October 1994, 'HAs to police fundholding'.

[13] *Hospital Plan for England and Wales* (1962) Ministry of Health, HMSO, London, Cmnd 1604.

[14] *Health and Welfare: The development of community care* (1963) Ministry of Health, HMSO, London, Cmnd 1973.

[15] *Report of the Committee on Local Authority and Allied Personal Social Services* (1968) HMSO, London, Cmnd 3703, para 32.

[16] *Social Trends* (1993), HMSO, London.

[17] Letter from Andrew Foster and Herbert Laming to health and social services authorities and trusts: EL(92)65/CI(92)30, September 1992.

[18] Letters from Alan Langlands and Herbert Laming: EL(93)18 (March 1993) and EL(93)119 (December 1993).

[19] *Implementing Community Care: Population needs assessment. Good practice guidance* (1993) Price Waterhouse/Department of Health, London.

[20] *Community Care Plan 1992–93* London Borough of Hammersmith.

[21] *Involving Older People in Planning and Evaluating Community Care: A review of initiatives* (1994) Social Policy Research Unit, University of York (funded by the Joseph Rowntree Foundation); *Involving Disabled People in Community Care Planning* (1994) Catherine Bewley and Caroline Glendinning, Joseph Rowntree Foundation, York.

[22] *Monitoring and Development. Analysis of a sample of English community care plans 1993/94* (1993) Brian Hardy, Gerald Wistow and Ian Leedham, Department of Health, London.

[23] *Caring for People in Leicestershire. The community care illustrative plan 1991–92. Summary.* Leicestershire County Council Social Services Department.

[24] *Developing Managers for Community Care. Involving housing in community care* (January 1994) NHS Training Directorate.

[25] *Becoming Consumers of Community Care. Households within the mixed economy of welfare* (1994) John Baldock and Clare Ungerson, Joseph Rowntree Foundation, York, p 32.

[26] *Old and Clean* (1991), Age Concern Greater London, p 1.

[27] *Care in the Community. Definitions of health and social care. Developing an approach. A West Midlands study* (1991) National Association of Health Authorities and Trusts, Birmingham, p 14.

[28] *Continuing Care: Continuing concern* (1994) Martin W Shreeve, Association of Directors of Social Services.

[29] Described in a letter from Herbert Laming and Alasdair Liddell: EL(94)57/CI(94)20 (20 July 1994).

[30] *Becoming Consumers of Community Care*, Baldock and Ungerson.

[31] *Community Care in Transition* (1994) Lesley Hoyes, Rachel Lart, Robin Means and Marilyn Taylor, Joseph Rowntree Foundation, York, p 31.

[32] Ibid.

[33] Speech by Virginia Bottomley to Association of Directors of Social Services, 2 October 1992.

[34] *Caring for People in Berkshire. Community care plan 1994/95*. Royal County of Berkshire Social Services Department.

[35] *Creating Community Care: Report of the Mental Health Foundation inquiry into community care for people with severe mental illness* (1994) Mental Health Foundation, London.

[36] *The Times* law report 26 October 1993 and *Independent* law report 30 December 1993.

[37] *Diversification and the Independent Residential Care Sector: A manual for providers of residential care homes* (1993) Department of Health Social Services Inspectorate, HMSO, London; *Expanding Care: A practical guide to diversification for care homes* (1995) ACE Books, London.

[38] *Direct Payments for Personal Assistance. Findings* (November 1994) Social Policy Research 64, Joseph Rowntree Foundation, York.

[39] Department of Health Press Release 94/537 24 November 1994.

[40] *Being Heard. The report of a review committee on NHS complaints procedures* (1994) Department of Health, London.

[41] *R v North Yorkshire County Council ex parte Hargreaves* (1994) HC 30 and *R v Avon County Council ex parte* (1994) 2 FCR 259.

[42] *Disabled People Have Rights* (1994) John Keep and Jill Clarkson, RADAR, London, and SSI monitoring documents listed on pages 202–204.

[43] Based on Section 2, 'Setting Standards', from the Department of Health Social Services Inspectorate Caring for Quality publication, *Guidance on Standards for Residential Homes for Elderly People* (1990) HMSO, London.

[44] See the *National Assistance (Assessment of Resources) Regulations 1992*, Department of Health, London. Guidance on applying these regulations is provided by the *Charging for Residential Accommodation Guide*, which accompanied Circular LAC (92) 19 *Charging for Residential Accommodation*.

[45] Health and Social Services and Social Security Adjudications Act 1983, section 17(1), (2) and (3).

[46] *Commentary on Social Services Inspectorate Advice Note on Discretionary Charges for Adult Social Services* (August 1994) Association of Metropolitan Authorities, Local Government Information Unit, AMA, London.

[47] Circular LAC (94) 1 and *Advice Note for use by Social Services Inspectorate: Discretionary charges for adult social services* (1994) Department of Health, London.

[48] *SSI/RHA Community Care Monitoring. September 1993. National summary* (1993) Department of Health, London, para 11.2.

[49] Department of Social Security and Department of Health Memorandum to the House of Commons Social Security Select Committee, para 3.8, in *The Private Financing of Residential and Nursing Home Fees. Minutes of Evidence. Tuesday 11 June 1991*. House of Commons Social Security Committee, Session 1990–91, HC 421–iii, HMSO, London.

# Appendix 1

## The Disabled Persons (Services, Consultation and Representation) Act 1986*

### Section 1 (not implemented): Appointment of authorised representatives of disabled people

An 'authorised representative' is defined as someone appointed by or on behalf of a disabled person to act as such for the purposes of the Act. A local authority may appoint a representative for a disabled person who appears to them to be unable to represent themselves by reason of any physical or mental incapacity. The DHSS (as it then was) is given regulation-making powers for local authorities to do this.

### Section 2 (not implemented): Rights of authorised representatives of disabled people

This section requires the local authority to permit an authorised representative to act (at the request of the disabled person) as their representative in connection with the provision by the authority of any social services and also to accompany the disabled person to any meeting or interview in connection with the provision of such services. The authorised representative has a right of access to the disabled person at all reasonable times when they are living in a wide range of hospital or residential accommodation, including private residential homes and nursing homes. Initial arrangements are for representation in respect of social services, but the Act also allows these provisions to be extended to services provided by health authorities and to other services provided by local authorities.

* This summary is based on an undated summary of the Act by ACT NOW, the Campaign to Implement the Disabled Persons Act 1986, c/o RADAR, 12 City Forum, 250 City Road, London EC1V 8AF.

## Section 3 (not implemented): Assessment by local authorities of the needs of disabled people

This section requires local authorities (before they assess the needs of a disabled person for any social services provision) to allow the disabled person or their authorised representative to make representations as to their needs. If requested by the disabled person or the authorised representative, the authority must provide a written statement of its decision, specifying the needs accepted by the authority and the services it proposes to provide to meet them; or that in its opinion the disabled person has no needs; and the reasons for its decision.

If the local authority does not propose to provide a service to meet an identified need, it must also state this and explain the reasons why. There is a right to have the decision reviewed.

## Section 4 (in force): Services under section 2 of the Chronically Sick and Disabled Persons (CSDP) Act 1970: The duty to consider the needs of disabled persons

The local authority must consider the needs of a disabled person for services under section 2 of the CSDP Act, if asked to do so by the disabled person or their authorised representative or carer. (This duty is *extended* under the NHS and Community Care Act: if a person is deemed to be disabled, assessment must be made without the person asking.)

## Section 5 (in force): Assessment of disabled people leaving special education and Section 6 (in force): Review of expected leaving dates from full-time education of disabled people

(These sections are not within the scope of this book and are not described here.)

## Section 7 (not implemented): Hospital discharge of people with mental disorder

This section sets out procedures to be followed at and before discharge of people treated for six months or more for 'mental disorder'. The Government has said it will not implement this section of the Act, as provisions of the NHS and Community Care Act are an improvement on it.

## Section 8 (in force): Duty of local authority to take into account abilities of carers

This section requires the local authority to take into account the ability of a carer to continue to provide care on a regular basis when assessing the needs of a disabled person living at home. Carers are defined as those who are providing a 'substantial amount of care'.

## Section 9 (in force): Information

Social services departments are required to inform disabled people receiving any service from them of relevant services provided by the local authority or by any other authority or organisation, of which details are in the authority's possession. (This extends the CSDP Act, which refers only to other local authority social services.)

## Section 10 (in force): Co-option to local authority committees of persons representing the interests of disabled people

Appropriate organisations of disabled people must be consulted before an appointment is made to a body or committee of someone with special knowledge of the needs of disabled people.

## Section 11 (not implemented): Reports to Parliament

This section requires the Secretary of State to lay an annual report before Parliament on the development of community services for mentally ill and mentally handicapped people, the number of people receiving inpatient treatment for mental illness or mental handicap, analysed by age and length of stay, and other information.

# Appendix 2

## Acts of Parliament under which community care services are defined for the purposes of the NHS and Community Care Act

Community care services as defined in the NHS and Community Care Act 1990 are those provided under four Acts of Parliament.

## National Assistance Act 1948

Part III: section 21(1), as amended by the NHS and Community Care Act, states that:

It shall be the duty of every local authority . . . to provide:

(**a**) residential accommodation for persons who, by reason of age, illness, disability or any other circumstances are in need of care and attention which is not otherwise available to them;

(**b**) temporary accommodation for persons who are in urgent need thereof.

Local authorities 'shall have regard to the welfare of all persons for whom accommodation is being provided, and in particular to the need for providing accommodation of different descriptions'.

Section 47 of the Act provides for the compulsory removal from home to hospital or other suitable place of people for whom it is necessary to secure care and attention. These are people who

- are suffering from grave chronic disease or, being aged, infirm or physically incapacitated, are living in insanitary conditions, and

- are unable to devote to themselves and are not receiving from other persons, proper care and attention.

Section 47 describes the procedure for this.

# Health Services and Public Health Act 1968

Section 45(1) of this Act gives local authorities *powers*, with the approval of the Secretary of State, to make arrangements to promote the welfare of old people:

> An authority may, with the approval of the Secretary of State, and to such an extent as he may direct shall, make arrangements for promotion of the welfare of old people.

(In fact, the Secretary of State has never made such a direction, so this remains a *power* for the local authority, not a duty.)

Circular 19/71 described possible services to be provided under the Act, which could include:

- provision of meals and recreation;
- facilities or assistance in travelling to services;
- help in finding suitable households for boarding elderly persons;
- provision of visiting and advisory services and social work support;
- provision of practical assistance in the home, including assistance in the carrying out of works of adaptation or the provision of any additional facilities designed to secure greater safety, comfort or convenience;
- provision of wardens or contribution to the work of employing wardens on welfare functions in warden-assisted housing schemes;
- provision of warden services for occupiers of private housing.

# National Health Service Act 1977

Schedule 8, para 3(1) states:

> It is the duty of every local social services authority to provide on such a scale as is adequate for the needs of their area, or to arrange for the provision on such a scale as is so adequate, of home help for households where help is required owing to the presence of –
>
> (a) a person who is suffering from illness, lying-in, an expectant mother, aged, handicapped as a result of having suffered from illness or by congenital deformity . . .

Local authorities are also given *powers* in Schedule 8, section 2(1)(a) and (b), to provide other possible services for people who are physically or mentally ill, including: day centres, meals and social work support.

Powers were also created for the provision of laundry services in households where home help is, or can be, provided.

These services are included in the definition of community care services by the 1990 Act. Circular LAC(93)10 sets out Directions and Approvals for local authorities in carrying out their powers and duties under Schedule 8 of the Act.

# Mental Health Act 1983

Section 117 of this Act imposes a duty on the District Health Authority and the social services department to provide aftercare services for certain patients, in cooperation with relevant voluntary agencies. Such services must be included in the community care plan of the local authority.

This duty is described in the circular on the care programme approach (HC(90)23/LASSL(90)11), and in LASSL(94)4/HSG(94)27 *Guidance on the Discharge of Mentally Disordered People and their Continuing Care in the Community* (see pp 96–97).

# Useful addresses

**Action on Elder Abuse**
Astral House
1268 London Road
London SW16 4ER
Tel: 0181-679 2648

**Carers National Association**
29 Chilworth Mews
London W2 3RG
Tel: 0171-724 7776

**Counsel and Care**
Twyman House
16 Bonny Street
London NW1 9PG
Tel: 0171-485 1566

**Health Service Ombudsman**
Church House
Great Smith Street
London SW1P 3BW
Tel: 0171-276 3000

**HMSO**
Oldham Broadway
Business Park
Broadgate
Chadderton
Oldham OL9 0JA

**Local Government Ombudsman**
21 Queen Anne's Gate
London SW1H 9BU
Tel: 0171-222 5622

**Relatives Association**
5 Tavistock Place
London WC1H 9SS
Tel: 0171-916 6055

# Recommended reading

All Department of Health and NHS Executive publications, letters and circulars, except those listed in this book as published by HMSO, London, are available from the HMSO (address on p 197). Some titles listed in the References (pp 187–190) are not included in this reading list.

## General

*Caring for People. Community care in the next decade and beyond* (1989) HMSO, London, Cm 849 (White Paper).

Circular LAC(93)10 *Approvals and Directions for Arrangements from 1 April 1993 made under Schedule 8 to the National Health Service Act 1977 and Sections 21 and 29 of the National Assistance Act 1948* (1993) Department of Health, London.

*Community Care: Agenda for action. A report to the Secretary of State for Social Services* (1988) HMSO, London (Griffiths Report).

*Community Care in the Next Decade and Beyond. Policy Guidance* (1990) HMSO, London.

*Community Care: The Way Forward* (1993) House of Commons Health Select Committee 6th Report, Session 1992–93 HC 482–1, HMSO, Lonson.

*A Framework for Local Community Care Charters in England* (1994) Department of Health, London, and Joint Circular LAC(94)24/ HSG(94)47, Department of the Environment Circular 17/94 (1994) *A Framework for Local Community Care Charters in England*, Department of Health and Department of the Environment, London.

*Making a Reality of Community Care* (1986) Audit Commission, HMSO, London.

*National Health Service and Community Care Act 1990*, HMSO, London. (Part III of this Act is about community care in England and Wales. Part IV is about community care in Scotland.) Community Care (Residential Accommodation) Act 1992 replaces section 42(2) of the 1990 Act and amends subsections (1) and (1a) of section 26 of the National Assistance Act 1948.

*Policy Guidance* (as referred to in this book), see *Community Care in the Next Decade and Beyond*, above.

## Department of Health guidance letters on implementation

The Department of Health has written regularly to health and local authorities, describing monitoring to date, and setting out 'key tasks' – for planning and for other areas of the reforms. The letters are available from the Department of Health Store (address on p 197).

11 March 1992: 'Implementing Caring for People' EL(92)13/CI(92)10. From Andrew Foster, Deputy Chief Executive, NHS Management Executive, and Herbert Laming, Chief Inspector, Social Services Inspectorate.

September 1992: 'Implementing Caring for People' EL(92)65/CI(92)30. From Andrew Foster and Herbert Laming (as above).

14 December 1992: 'Implementing Caring for People: Assessment' CI(92)34. From Herbert Laming (as above).

15 March 1993: 'Implementing Caring for People' EL(93)18/CI(93)12. From Alan Langlands, Deputy Chief Executive, NHSME, and Herbert Laming, Chief Inspector, SSI.

23 December 1993: 'Community Care' EL(93)119/CI(93)35. From Alan Langlands and Herbert Laming (as above).

20 July 1994: 'Community Care Monitoring for 1994/95' EL(94)57/CI(94)20. From Herbert Laming and Alasdair Liddell, Director of Planning and Performance Management, NHS Executive.

## Community care plans

Circular 10/92 (Department of the Environment)/LAC(92)12 (Department of Health) *Housing and Community Care* (1992) HMSO, London.

Circular LAC(91)16 *Secretary of State's Direction – Section 46 of the NHS and Community Care Act 1990: Community care plans* (September 1991) Department of Health, London.

Circular LAC(93)4 *Community Care Plans (Consultation Directions)* (1993) Department of Health, London.

Circular LAC(94)12 *Community Care Plans (Independent Sector Non-residential Care) Direction* (1994) Department of Health, London.

*Community Care. Monitoring and development. Analysis of a sample of English community care plans 1993/94* (1993) Brian Hardy, Gerald Wistow and Ian Leedham, Department of Health, London.

*Implementing Caring for People. Population needs assessment. Good practice guidance* (1993) Department of Health, London.

*Involving Disabled People in Community Care Planning* (1994) Catherine Bewley and Caroline Glendinning, Joseph Rowntree Foundation, York.

*Involving Older People in Planning and Evaluating Community Care: A review of initiatives* (1994) Social Policy Research Unit, University of York (funded by the Joseph Rowntree Foundation).

## Care management and assessment

*Care Management and Assessment. Managers' Guide* (1991) Department of Health Social Services Inspectorate, Scottish Office Social Work Services Group, HMSO, London.

*Care Management and Assessment. Practitioners' Guide* (1991) Department of Health Social Services Inspectorate, Scottish Office Social Work Services Group, HMSO, London.

*Care Management and Assessment. Summary of Practice Guidance* (1991) Department of Health Social Services Inspectorate, Scottish Office Social Work Services Group, HMSO, London.

Circular LAC(92)27 *The National Assistance Act 1948 (Choice of Accommodation) Directions* (1992) Department of Health, London.

Circular LAC(93)18 *The National Assistance Act 1948 (Choice of Accommodation) (Amendment) Directions* (1993) Department of Health, London.

*Community Care Assessments* (1993) Richard Gordon, Longman, London.

*Getting the Message Across. A guide to developing and communicating policies, principles and procedures on assessment* (1991) Department of Health Social Services Inspectorate, HMSO, London.

*Hospital Discharge Workbook* (1994) Department of Health, London.

*No Longer Afraid. The safeguard of older people in domestic settings* (1993) Social Services Inspectorate Practice Guidelines, HMSO, London.

## Purchasing and contracting

Circular LAC(91)12 *Community Care: Review of residential homes provision and transfers* (August 1991) Department of Health, London.

*Guidance on Contracting for Residential and Nursing Home Care for Adults* (1994) and *Guidance on Contracting for Domiciliary and Day Care Services* (1995) AMA/ADSS/ACC, Association of Metropolitan Authorities, London.

*Purchase of Service. Practice Guidance and practice material for social services departments and other agencies* (1991) Department of Health Social Services Inspectorate, HMSO, London.

*Quality and Contracts in the Personal Social Services* (1991) Association of Metropolitan Authorities, London.

## Complaints

*Challenging Community Care Decisions* (1994) Public Law Project, Institute of Advanced Legal Studies, Charles Clore House, 17 Russell Square, London WC1B 5DR.

*Disabled People Have Rights* (1994) Final report on a two-year project funded by the Nuffield Provincial Hospitals Trust. John Keep and Jill Clarkson, RADAR, London.

*If Things Go Wrong . . . Access to Complaints Systems* (June 1994) and *If Things Go Wrong . . . Complaints Systems: Simplicity and speed* (July

1994) Citizen's Charter Complaints Task Force Discussion Papers Nos 1 and 2, Cabinet Office, London.

*The Inspection of the Complaints Procedures in Local Authority Social Services Departments* (1993) Department of Health Social Services Inspectorate, HMSO, London.

*The Right to Complain. Practice Guidance on complaints procedures in social services departments* (1991) Department of Health Social Services Inspectorate, HMSO, London. (Included with this Practice Guidance document is a booklet: *Complaints about the Social Services Department. Ideas for a practice booklet for clerks, receptionists and telephonists.*)

*Second Overview Report of the Complaints Procedures in Local Authority Social Services Departments* (1994) Department of Health Social Services Inspectorate, London.

## Inspection and quality

*An Inspector Calls. The regulation of private nursing homes and hospitals* (1994) Royal College of Nursing, London.

Circular LAC(94)16 *Inspecting Social Services* (1994) including Inspection Units Directions.

*A Framework for the Development of Standards for the Provision of Domiciliary Care* (1994) Joint Advisory Group of Domiciliary Care Associations, 6 Minerva Gardens, Wavendon Gate, Milton Keynes MK7 7SR.

*Gold Standards. Professional targets for the care of elderly people* (1994) Age Concern England, London.

*Guidance on Standards for Residential Homes for Elderly People* (1990) Department of Health Social Services Inspectorate, HMSO, London.

*Guide to Standards in Day Care* (1992) Age Concern England, London.

*Homes are for Living In* (1989) Department of Health Social Services Inspectorate, HMSO, London.

*Homes are for Living In* (1992 update) Department of Health Social Services Inspectorate, Manchester.

*Inspecting for Quality. Developing quality standards for home support services. A handbook for social services managers, inspectors and users of services and their relatives and friends* (1993) Department of Health Social Services Inspectorate, HMSO, London.

*Inspecting for Quality. Guidance on practice for inspection units in social services departments and other agencies. Principles, issues and recommendations* (1991) Department of Health Social Services Inspectorate, HMSO, London.

*Inspecting Social Services. Practice Guidance* (April 1994) Department of Health Social Services Inspectorate, London.

## Monitoring the reforms

*Community Care in Transition* (1994) Lesley Hoyes, Rachel Lart, Robin Means and Marilyn Taylor, Joseph Rowntree Foundation, York.

*Fit for Change? Snapshots of the community care reforms. One year on* (1994) Melanie Henwood, King's Fund Centre/Nuffield Institute for Health, London/Leeds.

*Monitoring and Development. A special study of purchasing and contracting* (1993) Department of Health, London.

*Monitoring and Development. First impressions. April–September 1993* (1994) Department of Health, London. Summary of first impressions, plus individual summaries of the following six studies in the *Implementing Caring for People* series:
*31st December agreements*
*Assessment procedures*
*Community care plans*
*People with mental health problems*
*Purchasing and contracting arrangements*
*Younger people with physical and sensory disabilities*

*Implementing Caring for People. Impressions of the first year* (1994) Department of Health, London. Further general summary plus individual summaries of the following studies:
*Care management*
*Community care for people with HIV/AIDS*
*Community care packages for older people*

*Housing and homelessness*
*It's our lives: Community care for people with learning disabilities*
*Residential care for older people: The F Factor/home and away*
*The role of the GP and primary healthcare team*
*Training and development*

*Monitoring Community Care: A review* (1994) Melanie Henwood and Gerald Wistow, Nuffield Institute for Health, Leeds.

*The Next Steps: Lessons for the future of community care* (1994) Age Concern England, London.

*Taking Care. Progress with care in the community* (1993.) Health and Social Services Bulletin No 1, Audit Commission, London.

*Taking Stock. Progress with community care* (1994) Community Care Bulletin No 2, Audit Commission, London.

*Towards Community Care: ADSS review of the first year* (1994) Association of Directors of Social Services.

## Paying for care

Circular LAC(93)6 *Local Authorities' Powers to Make Arrangements for People who are in Independent Sector Residential Care and Nursing Homes on 31 March 1993* (1993) Department of Health, London.

Circular LAC(94)1 *1. Charges for Residential Accommodation – CRAG Amendment No. 2; 2. Charges for Non-residential Adult Services under Section 17 of the Health and Social Services and Social Security Adjudications Act 1983* (1994) Department of Health, London.

*Commentary on Social Services Inspectorate Advice Note on Discretionary Charges for Adult Social Services* (August 1994) Association of Metropolitan Authorities/Local Government Information Unit, London.

*Discretionary Charges for Adult Social Services. Advice note for use by the Department of Health Social Services Inspectorate* (1994) Department of Health, London.

Joint Circular HSG(95)8/LAC(95)5 *NHS Responsibilities for Meeting Continuing Health Care Needs* (1995) Department of Health, London.

LASSL(94)10 *Preconditions on the 1995/96 Community Care Special Transitional Grant* (1994) Department of Health, London.

LASSL(94)11 *Community Care – Special Transitional Grant Conditions and Indicative Allocations 1995/96* (1994) Department of Health, London.

*National Assistance (Assessment of Resources) Regulations 1992*, SI 1992 No 2977, Department of Health, London. Guidance on applying these regulations is provided by the *Charging for Residential Accommodation Guide*, which accompanied Circular LAC(92)19 *Charging for Residential Accommodation.*

*Summary of Charges for Social Care 1993–1995* (1995) Association of Metropolitan Authorities, London.

## Involving users and carers

*Community Care and Empowerment* (1993) Phyllida Parsloe and Olive Stevenson, Joseph Rowntree Foundation/Community Care, York.

*Implementing Community Care. Informing users and carers* (1993) Department of Health, London.

*Information on Community Care post April '93. The concerns of users and carers. Summary of observations by the National Users and Carers Group* Department of Health, London.

*Putting People First. Consumer consultation and community care* (1990) Discussion paper, Welsh Consumer Council, Castle Buildings, Womanby Street, Cardiff CF1 2BN.

*Squaring the Circle: User and carer participation* (1993) K Ellis, Joseph Rowntree Foundation/Community Care, York.

*User Involvement in Social Services. An annotated bibliography* (1992) Tessa Harding and Angela Upton, National Institute for Social Work, London.

*User Panels: New ways of working* (1994) and *User Panels: Seeking representative views from frail older people* (1994) M Baines, J Cormie and M Crichton, Age Concern Scotland, Edinburgh.

## Training

NHS Training Directorate: to date they have published 13 titles on implementing the reforms. Subjects covered include involving general practitioners, inter-agency development, involving users and carers, and joint commissioning. For further information contact NHS Training Directorate, St Bartholomew's Court, 18 Christmas Street, Bristol BS1 5BT. Tel: 0177 929 1029.

*Training for the Future. Training and development guidance to support the implementation of the NHS and Community Care Act 1990 and the full range of community care reforms* (1993) Department of Health, London.

## Other useful reading

*Community Life: A code of practice for community care* (1990) Centre for Policy on Ageing, London.

*Home Help and Care: Rights, charging and reality* (1992) Evelyn McEwen, Age Concern England, London.

*Housing: The foundation of community care* (1989) Alison Wertheimer, NFHA/MIND, London. 2nd edition.

*The Last Refuge* (1962) Peter Townsend, Routledge and Kegan Paul, London.

*Mentally Incapacitated Adults and Decision Making: A new jurisdiction* (1993) Law Commission, HMSO, London.

*Put Away: A sociological study of institutions for the mentally retarded* (1969) Pauline Morris, Routledge and Kegan Paul, London.

*Race Relations Code of Practice in Primary Health Care Services for the Elimination of Racial Discrimination and the Promotion of Equal Opportunities* (1992) Commission for Racial Equality, London.

*Report of a Study on Community Care* (1981) Department of Health and Social Security, London.

*Residential Care: A positive choice. Report of the independent review of residential care* (1988) Chaired by Gillian Wagner, HMSO, London (Wagner Report).

*Working for Patients* (1989) HMSO, London, Cm 55 (White Paper).

# About Age Concern

*The Community Care Handbook* is one of a wide range of publications produced by Age Concern England – National Council on Ageing. In addition, Age Concern is actively engaged in training, information provision, research and campaigning for retired people and those who work with them. It is a registered charity dependent on public support for the continuation of its work.

Age Concern England links closely with Age Concern centres in Scotland, Wales and Northern Ireland to form a network of over 1,400 independent local UK groups. These groups, with the invaluable help of an estimated 250,000 volunteers, aim to improve the quality of life for older people and develop services appropriate to local needs and resources. These include advice and information, day care, visiting services, transport schemes, clubs, and specialist facilities for physically and mentally frail older people.

**Age Concern England**
1268 London Road
London SW16 4ER
Tel: 0181-679 8000

**Age Concern Scotland**
113 Rose Street
Edinburgh EH2 3DT
Tel: 0131-220 3345

**Age Concern Cymru**
4th Floor
1 Cathedral Road
Cardiff CF1 9SD
Tel: 01222 371566

**Age Concern Northern Ireland**
3 Lower Crescent
Belfast BT7 1NR
Tel: 01232 245729

# Publications from ACE Books

A wide range of titles is published by Age Concern England under the ACE Books imprint.

## Professional handbook series

**Carefully: A handbook for home care residents**

*Lesley Bell*

Recent legislation places increasing emphasis on the delivery of care to older people in their own homes, thereby underlining the crucial role of home care assistants. This accessible guide provides practical advice on the day-to-day tasks assistants encounter and addresses such issues as legal responsibilities and emotional involvement.

**£9.95 0-86242-129-2**

**Health Care in Residential Homes**

*Dr Anne Roberts*

With far more older people receiving care in their own homes as a result of the community care reforms, staff working in residential care are likely to encounter a greater concentration of residents with severe health problems. In a clear and straightforward fashion this book provides information on the common illnesses of later life and the medicines prescribed for their treatment and offers advice on what should be done in an emergency.

**£14.95 0-86242-156-X**

### Expanding Care: A practical guide to diversification for care homes

*Jenyth Worsley*

The business repercussions resulting from the introduction of the new community care system have led many care homes to examine the opportunities to diversify their activities. This handbook outlines some of the options – including the provision of domicillary, day and respite care – and offers advice on assessing local needs and marketing and tendering and explores the practical arrangements surrounding implementation.

£14.95    0–86242–154–3

### Old Age Abuse: A new perspective

*Edited by Mervyn Eastman*

Bringing together leading experts in this field, the second edition of this title examines current knowledge about the prevalence and causes of abuse, its diagnosis and treatment, and the training programmes which can be used to raise awareness of the issue.

(Co-published with Chapman and Hall)

£13.99    0–41248–420–X

## Money matters

### Your Rights

*Sally West*

A highly acclaimed annual guide to the State benefits available to older people. Contains current information on Income Support, Housing Benefit and retirement pensions, among other matters, and provides advice on how to claim them.

Further information on application

---

To order books, send a cheque or money order to the address below. Postage and packing are free. Credit card orders may be made on 0181-679 8000.

**ACE Books**
Age Concern England
PO Box 9
London SW16 4EX

# INFORMATION FACTSHEETS

Age Concern England produces over 30 factsheets on a variety of subjects. Among these the following titles may be of interest to readers of this book:

**Factsheet 6** *Finding help at home*

**Factsheet 10** *Local authority charging procedures for residential and nursing home care*

**Factsheet 11** *Preserved rights to Income Support for residential and nursing homes*

**Factsheet 29** *Finding residential and nursing home accommodation*

**Factsheet 32** *Disability and ageing: Your rights to social services*

## To order factsheets

Single copies are available free on receipt of a 9″ × 6″ sae. If you require a selection of factsheets or multiple copies totalling more than ten, charges will be given on request.

A complete set of factsheets is available in a ring binder at the current cost of £34, which includes the first year's subscription. The current cost for annual subscription for subsequent years is £15. There are different rates of subscription for people living abroad.

Factsheets are revised and updated throughout the year. Membership of the subscription service will ensure that your information is always current.

---

For further information or to order factsheets, write to:

**Information and Policy Department**
Age Concern England
1268 London Road
London SW16 4ER

---

# Index